SELLING to a SEGMENTED MARKET

SELLING to a SEGMENTED MARKET

The Lifestyle Approach

Chester A. Swenson

NTC Business Books

NTC a division of *NTC Publishing Group* • Lincolnwood, Illinois USA

Library of Congress Cataloging-in-Publication Data

Swenson, Chester A.
    Selling to a segmented market : the lifestyle approach / Chester
A. Swenson.
        p.   cm.
    Originally published: New York : Quorum Books, c1990.
    Includes index.
    ISBN 0-8442-3459-1 (softcover)
    1. Market segmentation—United States. 2. Consumers' preferences—
United States. 3. Consumer behavior—United States. 4. Life
style—United States. I. Title.
HF5415.127.S94 1992
658.8' 34—dc20   92-2698
                                                            CIP

This softcover edition first published in 1992 by NTC Business Books.
a division of NTC Publishing Group,
4255 West Touhy Avenue, Lincolnwood (Chicago), Illinois 60646-1975, U.S.A.
No part of this book may be reproduced, stored in a retrieval system,
or transmitted in any form or by any means,
electronic, mechanical, photocopying, recording or otherwise,
without the prior permission of NTC Publishing Group.
Manufactured in the United States of America.

2 3 4 5 6 7 8 9 VP 9 8 7 6 5 4 3 2 1

To my beloved wife, Joyce . . .
My greatest partner

CONTENTS

PREFACE

Stalin's secret agents were excellent information gatherers. Fortunately for the free world, those same agents were afraid to give him bad news or to tell him things that failed to fit the "party line". We live in the age of information, and that information tells us over and over again that the world is not what we thought it was twenty or thirty years ago. If today's corporate leaders wish to go beyond mere survival and win in this dynamic world of innovation, they must be prepared to go beyond traditional "party lines" to respond to the new and ever-changing face of business.

This book is intended for people who want information and are willing to act on it. It is written to provide a philosophical and practical basis upon which to build an intelligent response to the multisegmented marketplace. I have tried to convey the information in a concise manner, and hope that the reader will find it as interesting to read as it was for me to write. Today's business demands that its players act rather than *re*act to the challenges of the fast-approaching twenty-first century—the first several decades of which will be owned by businesses wise enough to respond to the segmented marketplace.

The intensity of everyday business sometimes allows us little time to express appreciation to those who make our successes possible. I am grateful for the opportunity to let all those people in my life know how thankful I am for their unfailing support and encouragement. No company is built by one person, any more than a philosophy of business is created by one individual. With this in mind, I would like to express my thanks to the following people for making this book and the business of segmented marketing a reality.

Special thanks must go to my wife Joyce and our daughters Pamela, Cheryl, Cynthia, and Erica for their constant support and encouragement. Thanks also go to the two fine young men I have helped to raise, Per and Eric. Without the indefatigable help of Linda Brown, who puts up daily with my changes in travel plans and organizes my business life, I would be lost.

To the many business friends and clients who read this manuscript and shared their comments, I also convey my thanks. I am also very grateful for the loyal backing of the staff of Marketing and Financial Management Enterprises (M&FM), whose constant study of the various market segments mentioned in this book and whose careful work in these markets supported my observations and conclusions.

Among M&FM's contributors, thanks go to Linda K. Moore, Rick Jacobs, Michael Broggi, Maria Theresa Mireles, and Roberto Trevino. My gratitude also goes to Bob Seagren (Olympic medalist and sports marketing specialist), Robert Cole, Tony Rhine, Bob Collins, and Bob Billingsley. Thanks also go to Bill Kay, John Parks, Susan Lowes, and Capi Fiola. Appreciation goes to Al Roberson, David Quick, Mike Garofolo, and Larry Kent—with special thanks to Dean Tyree Weider of Los Angeles Mission College, Al Marasca, Earl Martin, and Angel Martinez.

Burnet Brown's assistance on the energy issues section of this book was invaluable. My deep appreciation goes to Steve Falk, Hugh Hunter, Rod Davis, Art Arkin, Jack Sneddon, Gerald Kowitz, Larry Harrigan, and David Strole for their years of vision and support.

ACKNOWLEDGMENTS

The time and efforts of Arline Kaplan in the researching and production of this book deserve special attention. Arline's skilled professionalism and her tireless efforts were essential to the preparation, construction, and completion of the work. My appreciation also goes to her for the good cheer and winning spirit that made this book a reality.

A special note of thanks must go to my close friend, Gerald Fecht. Jerry gave generously of his time and expertise to make this a better book. A professor of marketing, he not only reviewed and critiqued each chapter, but helped me refine the key concepts of the book. He is a talented professional, and I thank him for his advice, support and guidance.

INTRODUCTION

When today's market segmentation experts speak, the corporate world listens. *Advertising Age* magazine touts "marketing by the slice"; conference promoters present the "how to's" of "winning in the regional marketing game"; and marketing prognosticators fill books forecasting the continued segmentation of monolithic mountains well into the twenty-first century.

It is with some nostalgia that I follow this growing endorsement of segmented marketing. When our marketing company was formed in the early 1970s, few companies had even heard of the term "segmented marketing." Even in the late 1970s, most corporate executives were unreceptive to the concept. They were convinced that the battle for market share could be won by spending millions of dollars on mass media blitzes or producing the most creative television commercials.

My own understanding of segmented marketing has been an evolutionary process. Early on, I noticed stark differences in corporate marketing strategies. I first worked for Security Pacific Bank. Because the banking industry was heavily regulated at the time, marketing issues were largely confined to the colors and designs customers wanted on their checks. From there, I moved into the highly flexible, creative world of the Walt Disney Studios, helping with their embryonic direct marketing business. Our mission: to sell Disney's record products to families with young children. We found that we had to do more than procure a mailing list of families with children; we needed to investigate what families did, what products they bought, and why they bought them. Inadvertently, we moved beyond demographics into psychographics and lifestyle studies. Armed with these insights, we then experimented with a variety of nontraditional marketing mechanisms—co-promotions with Grolier Publishing, ads in specialized publications, coupons, and Christmas stocking doorhangers—to win business.

DISCOVERING SEGMENTATION

After I made the entrepreneurial leap of faith into my own business, I carried with me a market sensitivity and interest in nontraditional marketing approaches. One of the first areas our firm entered was college marketing. In the late 1960s, college campuses were highly insulated institutions. Corporations knew there was a potential market behind those ivy-covered walls, but the gates were shut. When the Proposition 13 tax revolt hit the state of California in 1978, it sent tremors through the college campuses. The initiative cut property taxes in the state by 57 percent, severely limiting government spending in all areas, including education. Colleges began looking for alternative ways to support their programs, providing the programs would not be controlled or their integrity violated. We were one of the first companies to help build partnerships between colleges and such corporate sponsors as Adolph Coors Company, General Motors Corporation, and AMF Voit, Inc. We had to look at the differences between the college student and the general consumer and then identify the common interests of a college student in New York and one in California. From our experiences in the college market, we went on to work with Hispanics and many other population segments. All of this work was well in advance of the popularization of market segmentation. We have been on the cutting edge.

WHY SEGMENTATION HAS BECOME IMPORTANT

In the early years of our business, I found that most corporations had limited themselves to mass marketing strategies, and to some extent this situation continues today. Whole industries still rely on network broadcasts of NFL football and other sports to reach adult male consumers, despite the fact that the networks' share of the television viewing audience has been diminishing for years.

While mass media strategies are a necessary part of many marketing plans, it is dangerous to rely on them entirely. Such strategies are no longer as efficient or cost-effective as they once were in that the marketplace is changing. We have moved from a manufacturing-driven to a consumer-driven economy; the mass media itself is fragmenting; we are celebrating ethnic and social diversity, rather than pouring everyone into a homogeneous mold; and the growth rate of the population is slowing with a resultant impact on the demand for goods and services.

A CONSUMER-DRIVEN ECONOMY

When Johnny came marching home again after World War II and started a family, that family needed a refrigerator, a car, and other basics. But the United States soon began moving from a production-driven economy to an economy of abundance. The available supply of products and services far surpassed demand. To stimulate consumption, businesses began to create products and services which appealed to diverse groups of people with a wide array of tastes and values. We have become a Baskin-Robbins society, as John Naisbitt (1984, 260) so aptly describes it in *Megatrends*, where "everything comes in at least 31 flavors." The automotive market is an example. Compared to twenty years ago, there is increasing product selection. According to the Motor Vehicle Manufacturers Association, there were 109 different makes of U.S. passenger cars sold in this country during 1989. In virtually every industry, any company intending to introduce a new product needs to know to whom and how it is going to sell that product.

Many purchases today are largely discretionary. No one needs to buy a $60 tie; one can be purchased from a local department store for $12.99. No one needs to buy a $50 sweatshirt, when the local discount store has one for $10. So the issue becomes one of understanding potential customers—who they are, how they are changing, and how best to reach them.

MEDIA SPLINTERING

The whole idea of mass media and mass audiences is in jeopardy. Twenty-five years ago, it was rare for a family to tune into more than nine channels on the television set. Now, nearly nine out of ten can, and one out of three can receive thirty or more channels (Nielsen Media Research, 1988, 2). And network television's unabashed invasion of the American living room has been constricted by the ever-proliferating cable television systems, now more than 10,000; the widespread usage of videocassette recorders; and the creation of specialized networks. Sports enthusiasts can tune into ESPN, Inc., Hispanics have the UNIVISION and Telemundo Group, Inc., Spanish television and networks, and children enjoy the Disney channel. For a lesson in patience, go to a video store on a Friday night and join the long lines of people waiting to check out the latest movies. With more than half of all U.S. households owning a videocassette recorder, there will be no decline in the video store crowds.

Television is not the only mass media splintering into small fragments. In 1950, there were seven hundred radio stations; now there are nine thousand (Naisbitt 1984, 107). Peruse the magazines in a friend's home, and you may find that mixed in with *Reader's Digest* and *TV Guide* are *Golf Digest*, *Weight Watchers*, *Walking*, *Meditation*, and *Boy's Life*. In its listings of U.S. publications for 1989, Standard Rate and Data Service, Inc., cited 2,192 consumer magazines and five thousand business publications, many of which are "special interest."

THE MELTING POT MYTH

In the past, the emphasis in this country was on turning the "huddled masses yearning to breathe free" into homogenized Americans. When Israel Zangwill declared in his 1908 play that "America is God's Crucible, the great Melting Pot where all the races of Europe are melting and reforming! . . . God is making the American," he was espousing political rhetoric. That rhetoric helped ease the fears and hostilities of nativist Americans toward the newcomers, over a million of whom arrived in 1905, alone. Immigrant children were sent to public schools to learn English and "American" ways. My Swedish grandfather was certainly affected by these "homogenization" pressures. He would rarely speak Swedish because he was embarrassed and wanted to be thought of as an "American."

For some immigrants, these pressures led to an almost schizophrenic lifestyle:

"Between the world of our text-books and the movies and newspapers and the other world of our homes and parents there was a deep gulf; different interests, preoccupations, ideals, languages," journalist Eugene Lyons wrote. "On the threshold of your home you removed your American self like an overcoat, and you put it on once more when you left home." (quoted by Smith 1985, 132)

Inculcated in this melting pot mythology, most businesses placed ads in *Look* or *Life* magazine or ran commercials on NBC radio, either unaware or unconcerned that they were missing entire segments of the population.

In today's society, cultural and social diversity is not only accepted, but often celebrated. Ethnic, racial, and sexual barriers eased somewhat during World War II, when women, African Americans, Hispanics, and many other groups helped with the war effort. Then, in the 1960s and 1970s came civil rights, black power, brown power, feminism, and gay rights—all of which have heightened our sensitivity to minority concerns and social mores.

Not only is our sensitivity increasing, but our society is in the process of actually becoming more diverse. Between 1901 and 1950, most of the nation's 20 million immigrants came from Europe and Canada, according to the U.S. Immigration and Naturalization Service. But since the 1950s, this nation's ethnic mix has changed demonstrably. More than half of the 13 million new immigrants who entered the United States between 1951 and 1984 came from Latin America and Asia. The arrival of Indochinese, Cuban, and Haitian refugees, and the granting of amnesty to nearly 3 million illegal immigrants, primarily from Mexico and Central America, in the late 1980s has further increased the diversity. In at least three states—Hawaii, New Mexico, and Texas—the Caucasion race has actually become a minority race.

Even the foundation of our society, the family, is assuming new forms. The Ozzie and Harriet world, if it ever truly existed, is fading into obscurity. I grew up in a typical nuclear family: my father was the breadwinner; my mother took care of the house and the children. Today, more and more women are entering the work force, going to college, and starting businesses. And more and more men feel the need to share in parenting responsibilities, some choosing to be full-time fathers or share a job with their wife. An increased acceptance of divorce and nontraditional arrangements has led to a proliferation of different types of "families"—married couples with or without children, single parents (male or female) with one or more children, unmarried couples living together, blended families with children from previous marriages, and extended families with several generations living together.

THE POPULATION MYTH

Most industries believe that profits are guaranteed by an expanding population. If consumers are growing in numbers, obviously, there will be more people purchasing products or services; the future is secure. And the fact is that until the mid-1970s, natural population growth made marketing easy. But times have changed. The U.S. population is growing just under one percent per year, and each year the rate of growth diminishes slightly. It is highly unlikely that most companies or their shareholders will be content with a sales or profit growth of less than one percent per year.

All of these societal trends present major marketing challenges. To meet these challenges companies must consider capturing consumers segment by segment and securing the fastest-growing segments before competitors do.

INTERNATIONAL MARKETS

Moving from mass marketing to segmentation may require some major shifts in corporate thinking and operations, but it is segmentation that supports companies in global marketing.

Much of what I learned about market segmentation came from my travels throughout Europe. It is quite apparent that Italians are not like the English, Irish, Swedes, Germans, or Spaniards. European marketers have a much better grasp of segmented marketing. One of the mistakes that many U.S. companies make when they go abroad is that they have little empathy for foreign cultures and try to do mass merchandizing. This does not work! In *Thriving on Chaos*, Tom Peters (1988, 124) warns American firms that "catering to local tastes, not so-called global branding (one kind of tomato soup for 125 countries), is essential." He (1988, 130) cites examples of how Coca-Cola took the lime taste out of Sprite to cater to the Japanese, while Pizza Hut added jalapeños to its available pizza toppings in Mexico.

The segmentation guidelines presented in this book may serve companies well when doing business internationally. Whether selling products and services in Europe, Asia, Africa, or the United States, a good marketer understands differences in culture, history, attitudes, values, and preferences, and then markets to those differences.

SEGMENTATION AND
THE LIFESTYLE APPROACH

At a time when mass marketing was still in the ascendancy, Wendell Smith wrote in the *Journal of Marketing* (July 1956, 4) of the need to target homogeneous components of a heterogeneous market rather than the market as a whole. He called this strategy "segmentation," explaining that it was designed for a "heterogeneous market by emphasizing the precision with which a firm's products can satisfy the requirements of one or more distinguishable market segments."

Of course, it took a considerable amount of time before his theory caught on. But companies are finding that segmented marketing enables them to increase their market share or even discover hidden markets. Consider the case of Reebok International, which went from $1.3 to $900 million in athletic footwear sales in just a few years. According to Angel Martinez, a vice president, Reebok relied on intuition, observation, and one-on-one conversations with retailers and potential customers and discovered a hidden, but very large market segment—women. "We didn't take market share from anyone," Martinez explains. "We just created a vast, new marketing opportunity" (Martinez, 1988 15).

While some companies make tremendous gains through the use of market segmentation techniques, others lose substantial market shares because they are blinded by success and are interested only in fail-safe programs. In the past, most car manufacturers would not even introduce a new model unless it was expected to sell at least a half million. International Business Machines Corporation (IBM) would not bother to enter a market lacking a potential sales value of at least $100 million. These attitudes, common to many large corporations, made it easy for smaller companies to consume the elephant, one bite at a time. If IBM has recognized the potential of personal computers, it is unlikely that companies such as Apple Computer would have ever gained a foothold. Now Apple with its Macintosh is challenging IBM on its own business computer turf. Similarly, Reebok never would have achieved such massive growth if Nike and Adidas had emphasized the women's market.

Learning from the errors of others, several large U.S. corporations are implementing segmentation strategies. Campbell Soup Company is pursuing regional markets, while Anheuser-Busch, Inc., and Metropolitan Life Insurance are going after Hispanic segments. Besides pursuing its traditional youth market, Coca-Cola USA is courting African Americans and Hispanics who represent 23 percent of the company's consumers.

When the concept of segmentation is applied to a mass market, the forms it takes are limited only by the imagination of the segmenter and the potential and accessibility of the selected market segment. Not only can consumers be segmented by age, sex, race, income, household size, education, and other demographic or socioeconomic characteristics; they can also be segmented by where they live, their buying behavior, their self-concepts, personality traits, and emotional needs, and their attitudes, interests, opinions, activities, and organizational memberships.

While this book focuses on consumer market segments, segmentation can be applied to industrial markets as well. Here the bases of segmentation might be type of industry, geographic trade area, and financial factors.

HOT MARKETS

More articles in the trade and consumer press are appearing on Hispanic purchasing power, minority markets, the booming business of aging, and women. These articles are harbingers of our country's economic future.

Women comprise the largest submarket in the country, and their buying power is increasing as their education level and income edge up to men's. Women used to make 60 percent of men's hourly wages; today they make 70 percent, according to the *Cosmopolitan Report on the Changing Life Course of American Women* (McLaughlin and Zimmerle 1988, 7).

One of the major areas for market growth is the burgeoning minority populations. Hispanics are the fastest growing segment. From 1980 to 1988, this group increased by approximately 34 percent (4.8 million), compared to only 7 percent for the non-Hispanic population. By the year 2000, Hispanics could number 31.2 million and comprise 10 percent of the U.S. population. African Americans, now numbering some 30.7 million, represent the largest minority in the nation; by the year 2000, they are expected to number 35 million, representing 13 percent of the population. Asian Americans and other races, now numbering 8.6 million, are expected to reach 11.6 million by the year 2000 and represent 4.3 percent of the population. Combining Hispanics, African Americans, and other races, by the year 2000, minorities will comprise more than one-fourth of the population.

African Americans currently are a $240-billion market according to recent surveys (Shriver 1989, TV-1). Strategy Research Corporation (1989, 5) estimates Hispanic buying power at $171.1 billion for 1989. And the Asian-American market is estimated at about $35 billion (Westerman 1989, 28).

A segment that has both economic clout and numbers is today's older generation. These individuals control more than three-fourths of the nation's financial assets and half its spending power. One in five Americans is 55 years of age or older, and in fifteen or twenty years baby boomers will swell their ranks to 85 million, 29 percent of the population.

Along with these key segments, there are smaller, emerging, and influential segments which merit attention: college students, military personnel and their families, gays, and the "greens" (activists on environmental issues).

America's colleges and universities represent a market of 12.5 million students, a market equal to the population of Southern California. Not only do college students spend about $20 billion on discretionary purchases, ranging from toiletries to tennis shoes, according to the College Stores Research and Educational Foundation (October 1986, 1), but they influence high school students, their parents, and society at large.

THE REALITY OF SEGMENTATION

While many segments are attractive markets, some fundamental truths must be recognized before a company embarks on segmentation strategies.

Moving Targets

Researchers may record a segment as married couples between 25 and 29 years old with one and one-half children, half a cat, and half a dog, living in a three-bedroom, two-bath home. But the reality is that these are moving targets. It is essential to go beyond the static demographic outline to record what is happening in consumers' lives. The women of today, for instance, bear little resemblance to the women of the 1950s. They are joining the labor force in record numbers, filling the colleges, and competing for blue-collar and white-collar jobs which were once male bastions. Many career women are becoming mothers for the first time after the age of 30.

Thomas Jefferson once warned that the price of liberty is eternal vigilance. Similarly, the price of success in business requires constant attention. At best, we can look at the present and past to see if we can make an educated guess as to where the consumer segment is heading in the future. But we are not soothsayers, and sometimes the best-laid plans of mice, men, and marketers go awry.

Segments within Segments

Beneath the surface of the Asian-American segment are Chinese, Koreans, Vietnamese, Filipinos, and Japanese—all maintaining their relative autonomy within a larger framework. The Hispanic market, too, is multifaceted, consisting of Mexicans, Puerto Ricans, Cubans, Haitians, Jamaicans, Dominicans, South Americans, and Central Americans. And moving beyond attitudinal differences of feminists and traditionalists, the women's market can be divided into numerous subsegments, including professionals, housewives, working mothers, and single mothers.

When formulating marketing plans to reach particular segments, a company needs to recognize that approaches which work for one subsegment may not work for another, particularly if there is a difference in language or culture.

Cross-Overs

Life with consumer segments is not always black or white. In fact, black and white men are likely to share common interests in football, basketball, and track. Americans of European ancestry are eating sushi and tacos, while Hispanics enjoy pizza and hamburgers. The moral of these examples is that consumer segments are not tightly discrete or distinct. Segmentation, then, becomes a sophisticated process of fine-tuning.

The Multiplier Effect

The dynamics of the marketplace reveal that college students influence other teenage consumers and children—barely old enough to remember the tune of their favorite commercial— influence their parents. Obviously, segments affect each other.

When the multiplier effect results in increased sales for a company, it is great. Certainly, Reebok prospered when the women consumers it had carefully nurtured through aerobics began to influence their husbands and boyfriends to buy from the footwear manufacturer. But beware the downside. In the 1970s Adolph Coors Company became ensnared in a controversy over hiring and employee promotion practices. Hispanics, women, and other consumer segments joined the AFL-CIO's boycott of the company, and the road back to winning these segments was a long and expensive ordeal.

IS IT WORTH IT?

Obviously, implementing segmentation strategies is not for the naive or the reckless. The increasing complexities of the U.S. marketplace require increasing sophistication in the research and analysis of segments and in the implementation of segmented marketing programs. But the projected benefits are well worth the effort.

New Opportunities

Psalm 118:22 says that "the stone which the builders refused is become the head stone of the corner." Sam M. Walton, named by *Forbes* magazine as the richest man in the United States, became so by making rural America his cornerstone. Sears, Roebuck and Company and K Mart Corporation were not serving the needs of small towns, but Walton saw communities with populations of 50,000 or less as a viable market. He opened his first Wal-Mart in Rogers, Arkansas, in 1962, and now has some 1,100 Wal-Mart Discount City stores clustered in the Mississippi Valley and the Gulf Coast states. Sharing rural American values, Walton based the company's growth on small-town friendliness, a loyalty toward American-made goods, and a willingness to offer his customers good prices without surcharging them because they lived in small towns. Walton employed a geographic segmentation strategy and won for himself a highly profitable market.

Many entrepreneurial companies owe their success to market segmentation strategies. For instance, a group of students at the University of Southern California noticed that an increasing number of the students on campus were women. They realized that while there were innumerable calendars featuring shapely young women targeted toward a male audience, nothing similar existed for women. These young entrepreneurs then produced the Looking Good Calendar featuring sexy male models and aimed it right at the walls of college coeds. Their strategy has netted them substantial profits.

Improving Market Share

Finding itself embroiled in what one observer has called the "beer wars," Anheuser-Busch Inc., used a segmented marketing strategy in 1978 to improve its market share against Joseph Schlitz Brewing Company and Adolph Coors Company in Texas. Working closely with local wholesalers, the company sponsored rodeo events in the north (traditional cowboy country) and Hispanic band tours in the southwest (home of large numbers of Mexican Americans). Because of these and other programs, Anheuser-Busch captured the top beer sales position in the state.

Meeting Consumer Preferences

In *The Third Wave*, Alvin Toffler warned that the "mass market has split into ever-multiplying, ever-changing sets of mini-markets that demand a continually expanding range of options . . . " (Toffler 1980, 248). Staying competitive means being able to develop and refine products and services to meet that segment's needs and preferences. Denny's Restaurants, for example, has regionalized its chili recipe. Its basic sweet chili is warmed up for Californians, who like their chili with onions, sour cream, and salsa, while local recipes are used in Cincinnati, Texas, and Chicago.

Outmaneuvering the Competition

Many consumer segments are virginal in the sense that the corporate world has not paid attention to them. But, by pursuing a specific segment and becoming an ally with it, a company can quickly secure its market position before potential competitors notice. When Reebok first entered the marketplace, it certainly was not a household word. By quietly targeting women, it created a brand name in six years and achieved an enviable leadership position in the aerobics shoe market. Similarly, Topol toothpaste carved out a profitable share of the toothpaste market by targeting smokers with discolored teeth before other toothpaste manufacturers entered the fray.

Dollar Savers

While "Get more bang for your buck" may be a cliché, it is also one of the most attractive features of segmented marketing. Segmentation enables a company to work with organizations, special interest magazines, and cable television and radio shows which reach specific segments rather than waste dollars on a shot-gun mass media approach which will hit many non-buyers as well as potential customers.

Business Week's marketing editor, Mark Vamos, warns that "the wasteful days of ever-increasing spending" on mass marketing methods are over (*Marketing News* 1987, 22).

National or Local—No Problem

In recent years, the Big Three automakers have implemented specific programs aimed at such key segments as women professionals, the military, Hispanics, and college students. On the regional level, automobile dealerships are attracting college-age customers through their cooperatively sponsored campus programs. In San Francisco, a Volkswagen dealer has built his business primarily through appealing to the Asian-American middle class. He has placed ads in the Chinese language Yellow Pages and sends his salespeople out to visit shops frequented by Asian Americans (Kotkin 1987, 46). Regardless of whether a business is nationwide, regional, or local, segmented marketing techniques can work efficiently and effectively.

THE NECESSITY OF THE LIFESTYLE APPROACH

Many Fortune 500 corporations have vaults of research about their target segments. Not long ago, companies armed with such extensive data had a significant competitive advantage. But the explosion of information has all but eliminated this edge. Most of the statistics and data are readily available or easily obtainable. Marketing-oriented publications contain a barrage of ads from research organizations promising race and ethnic data by zip codes, surveys, geographic data bases, economic and demographic data by county, ad infinitum. Along with the proliferation of research organizations, business and marketing majors are being meticulously trained in marketplace measurement techniques.

But what comes after the research and academic training in measurement techniques? There is a missing element—the *how*. How must a company interpret information and creatively apply it to the marketplace to reach consumer segments in ways that attract their attention and they have not been reached before?

MEDIA CLUTTER

Reaching various consumer segments is no easy task in a media-saturated society where thousands of advertising messages inundate the consumer daily. The average newspaper reader invites six hundred new advertising messages into the home each time he or she brings in the newspaper. When that same person watches television and then gets into a car and listens to the radio, the number of advertising messages swells to two or three thousand a day (Smith 1988, E-1).

If this saturation is not sufficient cause for most consumers to tune out, consider that they are also bombarded through direct mail, coupons, and telemarketers—both live and computerized, billboards, doorhangers, ads on their supermarket receipts and carts, commercials in the movie theater and on videos, and even electronic messages on blimps. The numbers are staggering. A decade or so ago, 27.6 billion cents-off coupons were distributed each year. Now, Manufacturers Coupon Control Center estimates that some 215.2 billion coupons are distributed annually. In a year's time, an estimated 52.8 billion direct mail pieces are shipped (*Forbes* 1985, 123)—that is 223 pieces for every man, women, and child in the United States. The effect of this clutter is to create an attention deficit among audiences. More than half of all viewers surveyed say they pay less or no attention to commercials (Lazarus 1988, 2).

SOPHISTICATED CONSUMERS

Consumers are becoming more sophisticated, more protected, and less naive about advertising techniques. Approaches which worked well a decade ago have little or no impact today. Educated working women can no longer be reached through marketing approaches that play on the guilt of not having a spotlessly clean home. Even the once-trusted banking industry is viewed with a jaundiced eye. A recent study conducted by Consumer Network of Philadelphia found that consumers see bank advertising as not very informative and only somewhat honest.

Consumers are also becoming more elusive, with their attention diverted in a multitude of directions. In our household, "couch potato" is a foreign word. I am busy with my business concerns and getting my kids through college; my wife is completing work on her bachelor's degree as well as managing our household; and my kids are teenagers and young adults, need

I say more. When it comes to accessibility through the mass media, entire segments of consumers are equally elusive. College students, for instance, watch very few hours of television a week compared to the average viewer. Children may use television for background noise while studying. At other times, they have the uncanny knack of watching two programs simultaneously.

THE LIFESTYLE APPROACH

Given the drastically changed marketplace and the challenge of getting in, through, or around the media clutter, what can be done? It is time to go beyond traditional marketing techniques, beyond mass media advertising as a sole solution, beyond conventional market research, and beyond equating marketing efficiency with costs per thousand.

What is required is a rethinking about marketing, a laserlike focus on consumer segments, and a pursuit of these segments using a marketing mix that includes long-term, relationship-building, grass-roots programs. I call this approach lifestyle marketing. The lifestyle approach is aggressive, active, high-touch marketing. It takes a company into the community where it talks *with* members of a target segment, not *at* them.

The foundation of the lifestyle approach is that each market segment has certain "points of commonality." These points can include shared values and concerns; preferred recreational activities; common membership in clubs, organizations, and institutions; ethnic and religious connections; heroes and role models; a shared generational experience, such as the Depression or World War II; or a geographical loyalty. For most Hispanics, a point of commonality is the Catholic Church; for older Americans, it is often their penchant for travel; and for college students, it could be their participation in intramural sports.

A company using the lifestyle approach identifies the points of commonality for its target consumer segments and then affiliates with esteemed individuals, organizations, and activities that embody these points of commonality. These affiliations may be with recreational and sports organizations, schools and alumni associations, or church social networks—whatever vehicles most effectively take the company's product line or service and its message into the community for a face-to-face encounter with the consumer. By becoming a friend to those consumer segments, a company enters their "circle of trust" and is viewed and responded to differently than other companies who merely advertise. To understand the essence of this approach, place yourself in the role of a consumer. If a stranger comes to your front door and just stands there, it is unlikely that you will invite that person into your home; but if a friend stops by with a message for you, you will usually invite the friend in to sit down and have a cup of coffee, and listen to the message.

BENEFITS OF THE LIFESTYLE APPROACH

Viva Your Difference!

In today's competitive marketplace, there is less perceived differentiation among similar products and services. If a company's product or service and that of its competitor's is equally good and similarly priced, what is the basis for a consumer's selection? By identifying key consumer segments, understanding what motivates them, and working on creating an affinity with them through the lifestyle approach, bonds are created that may give a company a marketing edge. The reality is that increased consideration translates into increased sales.

The Halo Effect

In using the lifestyle approach, a company will often affiliate with key organizations that influence a particular segment, such as the Mormon or Catholic Church, service clubs, or nonprofit, cause-related groups. Since all these organizations have the right of refusal, their acceptance of an affiliation with a given company carries an implied endorsement. The company benefits from the halo effect. This implied endorsement is particularly valuable in winning trust among segments where a company might be perceived as distant or foreign.

Acing Out Competitors

In the mass media arena, there is practically an unlimited amount of time and space available for corporate action. Some ten years ago, for example, a pioneering chemical dependency program began advertising on television, urging family members to get their loved ones into treatment. Now the television airways are filled with advertisements of numerous treatment programs—all with similar messages.

By contrast, the number of organizations available for lifestyle marketing affiliations is limited. Consider the example of Subaru, which has built a "franchise" as the car of skiers and has enjoyed top import market share in several snow-belt states. Jerry C. Welsh, an executive vice president with American Express Travel Related Services Company and an originator of cause-related marketing, points out that Subaru, a Japanese car maker, became fully "Americanized" in the minds of U.S. consumers by supporting the U.S. Ski Team (Business Committee for the Arts 1986, 5). In the mid-1970s, we represented the U.S. Ski Team and negotiated that contract with Subaru. It was the first time an amateur sports federation permitted its athletes to be linked with a commercial enterprise. U.S. car manufacturers were approached with the idea first and turned it down. Mentally, they were still oriented toward mass merchandizing. In contrast, Subaru and its advertising agency saw a niche opportunity and capitalized on the ski team relationship to reach affluent Americans, many of whom ski. By becoming the "Official Car of the U.S. National Ski Team," Subaru also gained instant endorsement and name recognition in the United States and was able to graphically demonstrate the car's unique snow-handling characteristics to the "action crowd" most inclined to buy it. Since that time, Subaru has expanded the ski connection by sponsoring races and other ski-related events. The key point of this anecdote is that Subaru's affiliation preempts any of its competitors from doing likewise; there is only one U.S. National Ski Team.

Discretion

One of the dilemmas in marketing is how to pursue key segments without stereotyping a company's overall public image. It is in this area, in particular, that the lifestyle approach is highly effective. Suppose one of your consumer segments is Americans 55 years of age and older. You can develop a program with the Walking Clubs of America, many of whose members are over the age of 55. You can select a spokesperson for the program who is known for his or her good health, vitality, and integrity and who is respected by this age group. Such a spokesperson could be Dinah Shore or Ed McMahon. Then, you can promote the program through advertisements and publicity releases in such publications as *Modern Maturity* and *Senior World*.

Narrowcasting versus Broadcasting

As mass media costs climb higher and higher, more and more major companies rebel and look for alternatives through which they can maximize their marketing dollars. To reach smaller, targeted constituencies, it makes no sense to continue to spend millions of dollars on network television advertising. Suppose a company wants to reach the aged 55-plus generation. Rather than spending those often scarce marketing dollars to develop and air a commercial on network television, which would reach non-customers as well a target segments, the company can advertise in any number of magazines and newspapers targeted toward the older reader, sponsor walking and golf events, or host a monthly big band dance. Since dollars are not wasted on reaching non-customers, the return on investment is likely to be much higher using the lifestyle approach.

In Hispanic families the Catholic Church is a place of great trust—a source of spiritual sustenance and social gathering.

Placing an ad in the church bulletin may cost as little as $10 per week, yet that bulletin is read or distributed in church and often reaches 1,500 families.

Enhancing Mass Media Investment

Even if a company relies heavily on mass media advertising, the lifestyle approach can be an important adjunct. There is a synergistic effect. A segment that already recognizes and respects a company because of its involvement with its lifestyle activities will generally give more attention to that company's mass media messages. The messages also are more likely to be believed, since a trusting relationship has been created.

Many corporations include lifestyle programs in their marketing mix. Knowing that the youth segment is critical to its profitability, McDonald's Corporation not only spends millions on mass media advertising, but it also sponsors gymnastics events, has its name on a line of children's wear, and establishes Ronald McDonald Houses to help families with hospitalized children. Wherever its consumer goes, so goes McDonald's.

For the numerous consumer segments that drink beer, it may sometimes seem as if every time they turn around Budweiser is part of their lives. And their perception may be accurate. Anheuser-Busch Inc., in its "This Bud's for You" mass media campaign, targets several distinct consumer segments. Then it amplifies the thrust of its message through numerous lifestyle promotions designed to reach Hispanics, college students, military personnel, and blue-collar workers.

Share of Mind

In a rapidly changing marketplace, market share can evaporate unless a company has "a share of mind"—a favorable disposition toward its product or service. "Kleenex tissues has a share of mind," explains direct marketers Stan Rapp and Tom Collins in their book, *MaxiMarketing*. "It has been an old, familiar, comforting friend through laughter and tears, opening nights and last rites. It has a share of mind that can resist price competition" (Rapp and Collins 1989, 212).

Because of its personalized, "high touch" emphasis, the life-style approach enables a company to create a share of mind with its targeted segments. That share of mind can lead to not only impressive but ongoing marketplace results.

≫ **2**

GETTING THERE FROM HERE

Perhaps on many a harried executive's desk should be the sign, "I'm so busy, I can't hear myself think." Most marketing staffs are so busy filling up their marketing calendars and completing media and advertising schedules, they fail to stand back and think about where they need to go and what they really need to do to sell their product or service.

TAKING STOCK

When our company begins to work with new clients, we ask them to evaluate their existing marketing efforts against these criteria:

- How influential are particular consumer segments to the success of your product or service?
- Are your marketing efforts missing key consumer segments?
- What is the worth of specific consumer segments to your company both in the short range and long range?

- Are there segments you are unwilling to relinquish to your competitors?
- Can competitors duplicate your marketing efforts?
- Are you reaching key consumers in a personal, effective way?
- Is the audience you are reaching actually your consumers or are you paying to reach unqualified buyers?
- Are you using the same media mix as everyone else?
- Are you making marketing dollars go farther through tie-in promotions?

Their answers to these questions aid clients in recognizing marketplace changes which affect their business and in reassessing their existing marketing efforts.

MOVING BEYOND THE COMFORT ZONE

One of the biggest problems we encounter with clients is their allegiance to the familiar—the mass media—and their resistance to change. While the familiar may seem comfortable and safe, "business as usual" marketing is losing its effectiveness.

Fortune 500 companies and small businesses alike have painfully discovered that traditional methods may not always work. IBM spent millions of dollars on advertising for its PCjr, yet the product failed to get off the ground. A *Marketing News* story reported that Burger King's "Where's Herb?" campaign cost the company some $40 million with very little to show for it.

Humorist Will Rogers once said, "Even if you're on the right track, you'll get run over if you just sit there." In *Marketing Immunity*, George Lazarus rebukes entire industries for their complacency. He points out that until the late 1970s, the hotel business was booming. But when occupancy fell by 7 percent, the hotels were unable to generate new business. "They had not developed new ideas or programs to excite the marketplace," Lazarus explains. "And when they finally did develop those new programs, they all developed similar ones" (Lazarus

1988, 25). Children's clothing manufacturers are suffering from
the same disease. Back-to-school promotions, for example, are
the bedrock of the clothing industry's marketing strategies. Yet
with more children in nursery school, with summer and year-
round schools, and with working mothers less accessible through
the mass media, launching a once-a-year media blitz to promote back-to-school clothes is not as significant or effective as
it was even five years ago. Success in today's marketplace requires a willingness to move beyond "business as usual," beyond complacency and beyond imitation.

LOOKING BEYOND THE OBVIOUS

While working with Disney, I marveled at how he made his
living through the eyes of the child but the pocketbook of the
parent. Marketing was directed at children; children would then
convince their parents not only to take them to Disneyland but
also to buy them Mickey Mouse hats, Snow White watches,
and "It's a Small World" records.

Time after time companies miss this marketing dynamic. If
one relies solely on demographics, it would be concluded, and
rightfully so, that children one to 10 years of age do not have
the necessary income to go to Disneyland and buy toys and
other products. But children are among the world's "great per-
suaders."

Research on college students indicates that they have low
incomes, and therefore, are probably unable to purchase a car.
Looking beyond demographic research, however, one will see
thousands of late model cars jammed into the parking lots of
campuses. Obviously, someone is buying those cars, and in
most cases, it is not the parents making those buying decisions.

When we entered the college market, we discovered that while
students generally have incomes that would place them below
poverty level, almost all their money is discretionary, given to
them by parents and grandparents. We alerted automobile
manufacturers and dealers to this potential market, and many
now have ongoing, highly successful marketing programs on

college campuses throughout the country. The lesson here is to look behind the numbers and beyond the obvious.

ABANDONING PRECONCEPTIONS

Even more than teaching us to look behind the numbers, our experiences in college marketing taught us to avoid viewing segmented markets with preconceived ideas. Many car dealerships, for instance, conclude that Hispanics are not a viable market for new cars. By keeping an open mind, we found just the opposite is true. Hispanics have large, extended families. For a high-ticket item, such as a car, five or six working adults in the family will pool their money so that one member can get a car or pickup truck. And they will often buy with cash. Many come from countries where banks are unstable, so they are suspicious of banks and save their cash at home until ready to buy. The key here is to avoid eliminating an entire market segment on superficial evidence, but rather probe "how" its members buy products and services.

TUNING INTO DIFFERENCES

Frequently, executives and marketing staffs of companies will fly into a large city, say Los Angeles, attend scheduled meetings, eat in a hotel dining room or a familiar chain restaurant, look out at the city from their fifteenth-floor hotel room, and the next morning, fly back to their corporate headquarters. What a loss! How much greater their awareness of the changing marketplace would be if they rented a car and drove through Los Angeles and noticed the various ethnic communities.

The differences between ethnic groups, the differences between Michigan and California, the differences between baby boomers and retirees—all can present marketing and product or service development opportunities. On the other hand, failure to note those critical differences can lead to a loss of market share, not only to American but also to foreign competitors. Both the Japanese and Europeans are cognizant of and respectful of the differences in the marketplace. Certainly, it was Japan's willingness to honor those differences that enabled it to make major inroads in California's automobile market before Detroit woke up.

Fortunately some U.S. companies are catching up. To acquaint Polaroid executives with the Hispanic market, Filiberto Fernandez often takes company executives to Miami, treats them to Cuban sandwiches on Calle Ocho, the main strip in Little Havana, and takes them to Hispanic street festivals and into office building after office building where Spanish is spoken. "I could show them the research, but a picture is worth a thousand words," he explains (Lieblich 1988, 182).

WALKING IN THEIR SHOES

Several members of the American financial community have done remarkably well identifying what their potential customers want and value. They did more than analyze whether the potential customers had savings and checking accounts, short- or long-term CD's, and credit cards. Instead, they engaged in a process of "simply letting themselves live, as it were, in their customers' shoes, talking their language, thinking their thoughts, feeling their emotions, responding to their cues" (Levitt 1986, 134).

One result of such a process was Chase Manhattan Bank's Equine Card. The bank identified many people in its "wealthy" target segment as horse owners. To tie-in with their lifestyles, the bank created the Equine Card, a credit card program that included special equine insurance, discounts on equipment and health care products for horses, and a monthly newsletter.

No matter what the industry, walking a mile in potential customers' shoes can bring them right to a company's door. South Coast Medical Center in Laguna Beach, California, for example, recognized that expectant and new parents have a plethora of fears and questions. As a free service, the center created a Bear Beginnings Club to help parents who signed up to have their babies delivered at the hospital. Club members received regular newsletters on pregnancy and early childhood parenting, discounts on merchandise and services from local merchants, and a gift package from the hospital which included a stuffed bear and Bear Beginnings bib. Club members could also call a telephone hotline for answers to their pregnancy, childbirth, and hospital program questions and enroll in education classes including parenting/sibling classes, modified cardiovascular aerobics for women during and after pregnancy, and "Mommy and Me" classes.

FINDING COMMON DENOMINATORS

This process of "living in potential customers' shoes" involves both observation and step-by-step thinking. To begin the process, take out a blank sheet of paper. Start listing your target segment's concerns, attitudes, habits, affiliations, recreational activities, and heroes. Each of these items can become a point of commonality by which to create a bond with that segment.

Suppose you have developed a wall decorator product designed for the bedrooms of young children and have identified the parents as your target segment. After conducting some focus sessions to identify what kinds of designs appeal to children of that age, you begin the process of thinking through where parents go prior to decorating a child's room. Women make frequent visits to their obstetricians during the last trimester of pregnancy and to pediatricians during the first year of the baby's life, so you might have your product included as a wall decoration in their physicians' offices. Parents buy furniture in baby shops, where you could have your product prominently displayed. You might arrange to have a discount certificate for the product included in the gift package a new mother takes home with her from the hospital. Or you could let nursery schools use your product at a special rate, so that parents see it at the school. You might form an alliance with a local diaper company which issues discount coupons for your product. This word-of-mouth, grass-roots exposure can be augmented by advertising in specialized magazines and newspapers targeted toward expectant women and parents of young children.

What if your target segment is high school students? Build an alliance with the high school and get to know the school better than it knows itself. Find out which clubs are the most influential and sponsor them; support a homecoming activity; grant student discounts on your product or service; buy space in the school newspaper. Do whatever you think will work on a grass-roots level to let the students know you want their business. Be aware also that you are likely reaching not only the teenagers but their families and others in the surrounding community. For many people what is happening in their local community is more important than what is happening in the state or nation. In several states, for instance, high school and college football is as big as NFL football.

REDEFINING MEDIA

A necessary element of this thinking-through process is a willingness to expand the definition of media. Ask most executives what they define as "media" and they will tick off television, radio, newspapers, magazines, and possibly billboards. Yet the dictionary defines "medium" as a means of communication that reaches the general public and carries an advertising message. Acceptance of this broad definition opens the way for more creative approaches. Consider the approach of a California mini-truck dealer and his arrangement with a Southern California beach city. Financially strapped as many local governments are, the city needed vehicles for its shoreline lifeguard crew. The import dealer sold the trucks at below cost to the city with the provision that his name be displayed on the vehicles. The dealer thereby obtained exclusive exposure of his product before hundreds of thousands of beachgoers while simultaneously demonstrating the off-road performance of his vehicles—not an easy task in the heart of a metropolitan area. Similarly, Plough, Inc.'s Coppertone, which sells sunblock lotions, bought and painted trash cans and put the Coppertone name on them. As a donation to local seaside communities, it placed them on beaches. Other forms of media can include teenagers, marathon runners, and fitness walkers who wear T-shirts emblazoned with a company's logo. They are, in effect, living billboards. Even hot-air balloons and briefcases, floats and Frisbees, cups and calendars can be considered media when they carry a company's logo and message.

GIVING DUE RESPECT

In the 1970s, Frito-Lay's Frito Bandito showed up on the "unwanted list" of Hispanics who saw the cartoon character as demeaning. At about the same time, the restaurant chain, Sambos, dropped the "Li'l Black" from its name to avoid charges of racial prejudice. While these blatant stereotypes are now gone, there are other depictions which can still enrage an entire segment. Some Hispanics were offended by a fast food chain's commercial which showed a Spanish flamenco dancer accompanied by Mexican mariachis. Such incidences come across as silly and manipulative. It is unlikely that Hispanics would allow such an advertiser into their circle of trust, because they would likely conclude that the advertiser was seeking their business without bothering to learn about their culture and value systems.

It is vital to understand that minorities and women are often not sure as to whether a perceived rudeness was deliberate. If a white Anglo-Saxon goes to a bank and is treated rudely by a teller, the customer writes the teller's behavior off as rudeness. But if a Hispanic or African American goes to that bank and is treated rudely, that customer does not know if the teller is being rude or is overtly prejudiced. These same quandaries exist for minority viewers of advertisements or programs on the mass media; the only difference is that the impact of any faux pas is magnified.

When marketing to ethnic and racial groups, women and the 55-plus generation, it is important to recognize how sensitive these consumer segments are to any approach that seems prejudicial, condescending, or patronizing. Prejudicial action is not wrong simply because it is illegal, which it is; or unethical, which it is; or obsolete, which it is. It is also wrong because it is bad business.

Condescending or brusque sales and telemarketing staffs can also alienate these groups. It is amazing how much time and energy corporations devote to preventing employee theft, yet these same companies are apathetic about the loss of new customers due to the arrogant or uncaring behavior of their employees. Women in particular are tired of being discounted as serious purchasers.

A little sensitivity goes a long way. Consider the apparent caring demonstrated by Metropolitan Life Insurance Company which maintains a toll-free 800 number staffed by bilingual people, who can answer Hispanic callers' questions and direct them to bilingual sales and service outlets. Smaller companies with less resources can still convey a "we care" attitude. In San Francisco, a car dealer conducts Asian-American sensitivity training to alert his sales staff to cultural differences. He found that the Chinese prefer shopping in large family groups with the buying decisions usually made by family elders, so he trains his sales staff to address the elders even though the purchase may be for a younger member of the family. A caring attitude was one of the major reasons Disneyland became so successful. Walt Disney observed that people want to go to an outdoor entertainment center that is clean and where they are treated courteously. He created Disneyland to meet those criteria.

GETTING AN EXPERT OPINION

One way to avoid mistakes in dealing with ethnic, female, or older adult markets is to rely on experts, particularly if a company produces several different products and brands. Brand managers cannot be expected to be experts in several segments. A workable arrangement is to have the brand managers identify a number of products that might appeal to a specific segment. Portions of each brand group's budget can be cannibalized for the relationship-building process with a targeted consumer segment. A company insider with top management support can then convey priorities and budgets to consultants who know how to reach the segment. Such consultants should be people who deal daily with the targeted segments and who have a proven track record in building a successful relationship between companies and the segments they want to reach.

When working with college students, the military, and other affinity-group segments, consultants can also help a company avoid the "we know all about it" trap. Many companies, for example, market to today's college students based on the senior managers' own remembrances of what college was like in the 1950s and 1960s. They suffer from what I call "alumni myopia." Yet college life has changed dramatically. While most college students in the 1950s and 1960s stayed in dormitories and sorority or fraternity houses on campus, the majority of college students today commute. Generally the student body is older, with the median age of 23.8 years. Surprisingly, students are now much more conservative than their counterparts in the tumultuous 1960s.

CREATING WIN/WIN/WINS

"Do well by doing good" is a familiar platitude in the corporate world. But it also makes good business sense to affiliate with the clubs, organizations, and public and private institutions of target segments. Suppose you own a local car dealership in a college town. Have your representative approach the local alumni association and create a direct mail campaign over the signature of the association's president urging members to buy their next car from you. In exchange, you donate $50 of every sale to the college's scholarship fund in the name of the association and the dealership. This kind of program helps the college, makes the consumer feel good because he or she knows that the purchase will benefit the college, and establishes your company as a generous, caring, community-minded business.

Certainly, many sophisticated corporations marketing to ethnic segments make buying their products beneficial to that group. Coca-Cola bottlers, for example, established Hispanic college scholarship fund-raising programs. In each community, bottlers donated twenty-five cents to a scholarship fund for each case of Coke sold during a six-week period. The money was given to Hispanic organizations in each community to be awarded to deserving students.

Before affiliating with community groups and organizations, there are some caveats. A company must consider whether the organization meets the profile of what it wishes to project; whether the group or organization is well respected and well liked by all elements within the target segment; and whether the leaders of the group or organization will be cooperative. The company needs to know, for instance, if it can use officer names in marketing campaigns. Can it use the organization's mailing list? Will the company receive promotional mention at organizational events? It is frequently a good idea to use marketing professionals who have an ongoing relationship with such organizations to act as intermediaries. These professionals will have a sensitivity to the needs of both organizations and can act as a conduit. They can maximize the relationship on the company's behalf, but in a way that does not appear to be totally self-serving.

AFFILIATING WITH THE UPBEAT

The phrase from an old song, "you have to accentuate the positive and eliminate the negative," contains sound marketing advice. Be with your target segments when their defense mechanisms are down and they are receptive to your message. Join with them in their positive lifestyle activities: fiestas for Hispanics, or intramural sporting events and homecoming activities for college students, or wellness recreational programs for the 55-plus generation. The underlying guideline here is to affiliate with the upbeat, the festive, the meaningful in people's lives. Be part of their celebration, not their consternation.

SEEKING OUT THE INFLUENTIAL

In most businesses, and certainly in most advertising agencies, the conventional measure for determining marketing effectiveness is cost per thousand. Underlying the cost per thousand emphasis is the view that quantity is preferable to quality. This is faulty thinking. If a company spends $15 on a key influencer who in turn convinces five or six others to buy its product, it is cheaper than spending $5 per person to reach those six with mass media appeals. Working with influencers in any segment can be both effective and cost-efficient. A Japanese company introduced a new automobile designed to appeal to women with active lifestyles. Recognizing that aerobic instructors are usually attractive role models for their students, the company recruited aerobics instructors to help them launch the product. Obviously, this same approach helped Reebok become a major force in the footwear industry. It is like throwing a rock into a pond and watching the circles flow out from there.

LIFESTYLE AS LIVE THEATER

Many companies are used to buying time on network television, sitting back, and hoping for the best from their commercials. Nearly everything comes out as planned. These companies expect the same from direct lifestyle marketing programs. But there are differences which need to be considered. The lifestyle approach is the "live theater" of marketing and occasionally the unexpected happens—an outdoor event gets rained out or a celebrity guest arrives late. When working with volunteer community organizations, a company must be prepared to be patient, flexible, and work to enhance their activities. Some monitoring of these organizations will be necessary to achieve a company's objectives as a marketer. But the monitoring and increased involvement is a small price to pay for the extra mileage a company receives from working with these groups. Touching consumer segments in a personal way is much more effective than talking at them with a hard-to-measure thirty-second spot.

Frequently, there are unanticipated benefits with the lifestyle approach. Several years ago, a major automobile manufacturer decided to sponsor amateur soccer in the United States and enlisted the great soccer star, Pelé, as a celebrity tie-in for a college scholarship program. If the automaker continues to build upon its grass-roots support of soccer, it will benefit from the publicity bonanza associated with the World Cup of Soccer to be hosted by the United States in 1994. To exploit these unplanned opportunities that arise in the live theater of marketing, it is a good idea to set aside an opportunity budget. Suppose a company sponsors an inner-city youth boxing program and one participant makes the Olympic team. An opportunity budget gives that company the flexibility to capitalize on its windfall.

TAKING GRASS-ROOTS OVER GLITZ

When Chase Manhattan Bank and Rolex Watch USA sponsor squash tournaments to reach affluent consumer segments, it is a wise marketing move. Squash players and enthusiasts generally have advanced educational degrees and earn an average of $50,000 or more a year, so they are an appropriate target segment for the bank and prestige watch company. But frequently corporate executives opt for team or event sponsorships that have no relevance to their company's marketing strategy or target segments. These executives usually want to attend prestigious events or hobnob with glamorous celebrities as a boost to their own egos. They may ignore the fact that their target consumer segments prefer "blood and guts" bowling, tractor-pulls, or rodeos. Meanwhile, their astute competitor sponsors the bowling and tractor-pulls and moves right into their market. Certainly, grass-roots marketing is not very glamorous—watching the grass grow is not very exciting for fast-paced business executives. The payoffs, however, can be well worth the wait.

STAYING COMMITTED

When an established business discovers it is in trouble and losing market share, the usual response is panic, followed by an intensive search for quick-fix, one-shot programs that will immediately "move the needle." But the lifestyle approach requires a different perspective. It is a commitment for years rather than days, because the company is seeking to win a loyal consumer segment rather than a one-time purchaser. The relationship being created is not a one-night stand, but a marriage. Marketing plans and funding allocations that are organized on a one-month or six-month basis may have to be restructured to span five or six years.

Continuity is absolutely essential in lifestyle marketing to consumer segments. Too many corporations come in with token or symbolic involvements that can do more damage than good. If you cancel an ad in *Sports Illustrated*, the only person who knows you cancelled it is the ad salesperson. But if you are involved in a lifestyle-approach program for Hispanics, such as the annual Cinco de Mayo parade, and withdraw your sponsorship after a year or two, thousands of Hispanics, especially their leaders, will know. They will ask, "What did we do to hurt you?" or "How did we offend you?" If a company decides to reach into a segmented market, it needs to make a genuine commitment.

CREATING ALLIANCES

When two companies share the same customer profile, strategic alliances can be beneficial and cost-effective. Well-developed marketing alliances can assist a company in expanding its customer base. Such ongoing alliances should involve joint strategy meetings, a full marketing calendar, and cross-promotions in advertising. Of course, these alliances should be fine-tuned so that neither company is forced to take a backseat position. Equitable alliances are best when a trusted third party is brought in to execute the programs and ensure that both companies are maxi-advantaged.

Why enter into an ongoing alliance? Production, media, and marketing costs can be shared, resulting in substantial cost savings to both companies. Companies learn to trust each other and recognize each other's limitations and strengths; they come to know the key personnel in each company; and they achieve economies of time in that responsibilities are divided between both companies.

Consider the value of an alliance between K2, a manufacturer of premium skis, and Lincoln-Mercury. Despite their distinct industries, they had a mutual interest. They shared the same consumer segment—the upscale, 35- to 45-year-old age group. We worked with these automotive and sports equipment companies on a promotional alliance which enabled them to cross-market and increase their customer base. The program gave them reciprocal exposure at auto and ski equipment trade shows and gained Lincoln-Mercury's Merkur XR4ti, a turbocharged sports car, extensive exposure through a point-of-sale sweepstakes at 1,200 ski stores across the country.

Another example of such an alliance is that of Eddie Bauer, Inc., and Ford Motor Company. Eddie Bauer retail stores have a prestigious image in the marketplace and appeal to high-end customers. Ford secured a license to create an Eddie Bauer Bronco truck which has a specially designed interior and package design. Even though it is a small company compared to Ford, Eddie Bauer is very important in the minds of the affluent consumer segment. Through the alliance, Ford was able to differentiate the Bronco from the Blazer and appeal to the affluent consumer.

The principles of the lifestyle approach covered in this chapter are often painful lessons learned during many years of working with market segments. They will enable a company to begin replacing outmoded practices with relevant ones and to be well on its way to meeting the marketplace challenges not only of today but of the year 2000 and beyond.

SECURE ADULTS

When I started in marketing, few companies paid much attention to consumers aged 55 and older. Most businesses viewed older consumers as impoverished, inflexible, and unimportant, except possibly as a market for denture adhesives, hearing aids, and Geritol.

But these attitudes are fading, as companies are beginning to recognize that the profit streams flow from not only the youthful 18- to 49-year-old consumer segments, but also from the older generation.

Consider that older Americans:

- Represent a $900-billion market (Center for Mature Studies 1988).
- Own 77 percent of our nation's financial resources.
- Account for 50 percent of discretionary income after taxes.
- Have a median net worth of $60,266—nearly double that of the general population (U.S. Census Bureau, July 1986, 4).
- Account for $3 out of every $10 spent on consumer purchases, paying out $1 of every $4 on cosmetics and

bath products; $4 of every $10 on women's beauty services; $3 out of every $10 on food purchases; and $1
out of every $4 on alcoholic beverages (Berlow 1988).

• Account for 80 percent of all luxury travel purchases.

SECURE ADULTS

Because of their evident economic well-being, the 55-plus
generation can be identified as the "secure adult" segment. With
a lifetime of accumulated assets, freedom from child-rearing responsibilities and heavy mortgages, and supplemental monthly
incomes from Social Security, pension plans, or income property, most members of the 55-plus generation are economically
secure. Granted, many individuals fall below the poverty line,
but in the last twenty years, the number of Americans aged 65
and older who live below poverty level has decreased from 35
percent to 12.2 percent, about the same as for younger households. Overall, the United States now has the most affluent
secure adult population in the world.

To ignore the secure adult segment is genuinely a risky business, for it has not only prosperity but numbers—52.2 million
individuals. One in five Americans is 55 years of age or older;
in 1900, the ratio was one in ten. The U.S. population aged 65
and older is now larger than the entire population of Canada.
Furthermore, when the baby boomers start joining the ranks of
secure adults in ten or fifteen years, the numbers will climb to
85 million—29 percent of the population.

Another important fact is that the secure adult segment can
be viable customers for a long, long time—often twenty or more
years, since the average life expectancy is already in the 70s for
both men and women. And with the increases in longevity, the
number of Americans 85 and older will climb to 15 million by
the year 2050, five times its present size, while the number of
centenarians will grow from the current 46,000 to some 775,000.
If a company does not start reaching the 55-year-olds now, it
will be relinquishing potential market share to the competition.

MULTIPLE MARKETS

Despite its attractiveness, the older American market is tough to crack. People over the age of 55 cannot be lumped into one monolithic marketing category, even though many companies have mistakenly tried to do so.

The largest and most affluent subsegment of older Americans is the 21.8 million aged 55 to 64. Not only is their after-tax income higher than the national average, but they also have the highest median net worth of all households, buttressed by substantial home equity, interest-earning bank accounts, and investments in stocks and mutual funds.

Because of their affluence, these individuals are more willing to spend money on clothing, travel, entertainment, dining out, and other luxuries. In fact, some marketers have christened them "suppies" (senior urban professionals) or "opals" (older people with active lifestyles).

More educated than their parents were at the same age, this subsegment knows that they can extend their lifespan by participating in wellness and fitness programs and can live comfortably during retirement by engaging in strategic financial planning.

The 17.9 million Americans aged 65 to 74 generally are adjusting to new and different sources of income, spending priorities, and leisure patterns. The majority have quit working, so that income levels in this subsegment fall slightly below national medians. Many companies therefore conclude that Americans aged 65 to 74 are no longer a viable consumer market. Nothing could be further from the truth. The reality is that in 1984 the median net worth of Americans 65 to 69 years old was $66,621, and for those 70 to 74 years old was $60,573. These figures are nearly double the national average. Three out of four own their own homes and have interest-earning bank accounts, while about one in five have stocks and mutual fund shares.

Younger in attitude and more active than their forebears, most members of this subsegment live busy, fulfilling lives. With

ample leisure time and economic security, they travel, devote
their energies to numerous civic and charitable groups, and buy
luxury items they could not afford when they were younger.
Despite their vigor, the 65- to 74-year-olds have to contend with
the emergence of heart disease, arthritis, high blood pressure,
and other chronic illnesses, and they spend a lot on health care.
In fact, the 65-plus generation accounts for nearly one-third of
all personal health care expenditures.

For the 9.5 million Americans aged 75 to 84, there is not only
the challenge of preserving their health, but also of learning
how to live alone. The number of female-headed households
rises dramatically in this age subsegment; women outnumber
men two to one. More than two-thirds of the women are widows, and nearly half are living by themselves, giving rise to
marketing opportunities in the areas of safety, home maintenance, and the like. To cope with loneliness, many maintain
active societal and friendship networks and close ties to their
families. Economically, those in their 70s and 80s have income
levels that are about half the national average, but their median
net worth is still well above the median for all ages.

Until recently, people aged 85 and older were rarely studied
from a marketing perspective. There were just too few of them.
Now that is not the case. Such individuals number 3 million,
and this number is expected to double by the end of the century. Nearly three-fourths of this subsegment are women, and
their strongest needs are for health care and homemaking services. About one-fourth are in hospitals, nursing homes, or other
institutions. Nearly half have problems with personal care activities, such as bathing, dressing, and getting outside. And
they must often rely on others for help with homemaking, financial management, and driving. For businesses capable of
easing the personal care, home management, and mobility
problems, here is a ready market!

CONSIDERING COMFORT LEVELS

In *Age Wave*, Ken Dychtwald talks about the need to rede-
sign products, technologies, and environments to address the

physical changes of aging (1989, 311). It becomes harder for older Americans to read small type, to see in low light, and to differentiate between pastel colors. More than one-fourth of the over-65 population suffers from partial deafness, and many have increasing problems in their ability to move around. Companies need to design the operative side of a retail outlet with these considerations in mind. Food retailers might consider enlarging the type size of shelf-talkers and gearing their public address systems to accommodate the hearing range of older consumers. Automobile dealers might want to study how accessible and comfortable their dealerships are from an elderly person's point of view, possibly replacing stairs with ramp-ways and providing comfortable waiting rooms. Certainly part of building a trust relationship with the aged 55-plus generation is being considerate of their needs.

From this overview, it becomes obvious that secure adults are not the monolithic, uninteresting market that they have sometimes been judged to be.

SHORT SHRIFT TO STEREOTYPES

In an ad to promote its Golden Traveler Passport program, Continental Airlines showed two empty rocking chairs—one adorned with newspapers and glasses, the other with a shawl and knitting needles. The caption for the ad was "Another cliché bites the dust." This ad artfully played off secure adults' distaste for stereotypes which characterize them as being creaky or cranky, befogged or befuddled, stodgy or stubborn. Commercials and advertisements that portray them as "over the hill" are on the secure adults' hit list. While younger generations may have smiled at Wendy's "Where's the Beef?" commercial, older Americans were not amused and said so. Many felt Clara Peller's performance fostered the image of older people as eccentric and feebleminded.

One of the most difficult challenges in reaching secure adults is the age issue. In Madison Avenue's early appeals to this market, marketers naively tacked on the word "senior" or "retired" to advertisements and promotions, and congratulated themselves for their targeted marketing. Unfortunately, remnants of this mind-set continue. Ads for developers talk about "carefree retirement living" and "seniors getting more for less," while ads for restaurants promote "early bird specials for senior citizens" and "senior coupons." What is not realized is that secure adults do not perceive themselves as senior citizens; if you go to them with an "old folks" message, you will die in the marketplace. Numerous studies of the 55-plus generation indicate they are uncomfortable with such appellations as "senior citizen," "retiree," and "golden ager," seeing these terms as relegating them to an alien status in their own society. One older woman's personal ad typifies the resistance to age designations. She writes: "I am a young 63, white female. Hate the words 'senior and elderly.' I am a mature adult, professional, semi-retired. Have traveled around the world . . . "(*Senior World/Orange County*, February 1989, 39).

Not only are secure adults uncomfortable with age characterization, but they will lodge their complaint at the cash register. According to *Consumer Behavior of Older Adults—A National Survey*, one-third of the respondents said they have boycotted products or services because of inappropriate age stereotyping (Center for Mature Studies 1988).

Witness what happened when a major company introduced a shampoo for the "brittle, hollowed out" hair of the over-40 woman. The product struggled to survive in the marketplace until the company eliminated all age references from the ad (Alsop and Abrams 1986, 18).

So what does work? One of the favorite commercials of older Americans was the Coca-Cola classic spot. Art Carney portrayed a sensitive, positive man who obviously cared for his grandson. Another appealing commercial was "Golden Years," which showed an older man and woman meeting in a McDonald's restaurant.

Some marketers contend that if a company is going to use an age-based marketing approach, it must target *cognitive* age rather than *chronological* age. "If you ask older people how old they think they would be if they did not know their own age, about three-quarters of them give an answer that is 75 to 80 percent of their chronological age. Cognitive age—the age people feel—is what marketers should pay attention to," advises David Wolfe, founder of the National Association of Senior Living Industries (Wolfe 1987, 26).

LIFESTYLE APPROACHES

While cognitive age is preferable to chronological age, the most effective approach is to step around the entire "ageist mine field." It is safer to bypass an age-focus altogether and to target lifestyle affinities that will attract the attention of secure adults and draw them to a given product or service. Appeals built around health and fitness, self-fulfillment and enjoyment, social responsibility and involvement, and family are likely to capture their attention.

MAINTAINING HEALTH AND FITNESS

Committed to healthy longevity, today's secure adults are more concerned about maintaining their health than past generations. Health is, for the majority, their most valuable asset, and they will do what is necessary to keep it, whether it is using sugar and salt substitutes or playing golf twice a week.

In a 1987 survey conducted by the Daniel Yankelovich Group, Inc., more than half of the men and women 50 years of age and older acknowledged that they are paying more attention to watching their weight; eating more fish, poultry, and salads; watching their sugar intake; and using low-salt products (Daniel Yankelovich Group, Fall 1987, 11, 12).

One of the companies that has recognized the dietary concerns of older Americans is Campbell Soup Company. But rather than use an age-based message, its advertisements talked about Campbell's "Special Request" soups with one-third less salt than its regular soups. The ads ran in magazines read by older Americans. A similar approach was used by Kellogg's Company which urged *Modern Maturity* readers to "Get a Taste for the Healthy Life" with bran flakes and to send for a free book,

Game Plan for the Healthy Life, from former L. A. Rams/Washington Redskins coach George Allen.

Not only are secure adults generally more health-conscious than prior generations, they are also more physically active. Pick up a magazine targeted to older readers or your local newspaper, and you will find stories about 70- or 80-year-old marathon runners, 92-year-old Hulda Crooks who climbs Mount Whitney, and 72-year-old Shizu Lofton who teaches Tai Chi (Chinese exercises) to groups of people in their 60s, 70s, and 80s.

These older Americans are by no means unique. A national recreation survey conducted by the U.S. Bureau of the Census found that older people today participate more in recreation than their counterparts in the 1960s. Substantial increases were recorded for swimming, bicycling, and walking (Robinson, March 1987, 36-7).

Golf Enthusiasts

Anyone who has attempted to get a starting time on a golf course knows that one of the most appealing sports for those 55 and older is golf. In fact, the number-one sports market for 55-plus consumers is golf, according to a Sporting Goods Manufacturers Association survey. In 1987, secure adults spent $290 million on golf equipment and apparel (*Sporting Goods Business* 1988, 30).

Well aware that secure adults are a prime market for luxury car purchases, one responsible car dealership used golf as a vehicle to reach them. The dealership contributed a fleet of loan cars to a week-long Professional Golfer's Association tour event at one of the West's most exclusive country clubs. Public awareness of the PGA loan car program was magnified by a special sales campaign the week following the tournament when loan cars were offered to the public at discount prices.

Golf is also used as an entree to affluent secure adults by Florida land developers. One enterprising developer sent subscribers of *Golf* magazine a brochure featuring the championship golf course as part of his development (Edmondson 1987,

26). Others depict golfers in their ads or talk about country club living with such amenities as a golf course, pro shop, and PGA professional.

Walking

Walking comes close to golf as a favorite sport for secure adults. Fitness walking clubs are being organized all over the country; there are state-sponsored fitness walking competitions and cadres of sweatsuit-attired older adults who pace suburban malls as part of their daily exercise program. Among adults 50 years of age and older who participate in physical activities and sports regularly, 76 percent say they walk for fitness (Daniel Yankelovich Group, Fall 1987, 12). And not only do they walk, but they buy—$111-million worth of walking shoes in a year (*Sporting Goods Business* 1988, 30).

Seeing that $111-million opportunity, Reebok International contacted us, and we linked it with General Mills Corporation. Here was a case of two corporations with totally different products joining hands to reach the secure adult market through a program that recognizes how significant walking is to this segment. General Mills' Total cereal appeals to health-conscious older adults. On the back of Total cereal boxes, Rockport, a division of Reebok which manufacturers walking shoes, placed an offer for a free *Fitness Walking* book. The book was also followed up with an offer for a video, "Walk Your Way to Fitness," which could be purchased for $6.95. Appearing on the video were long-time NFL coaching great, George Allen, and other heroes with whom the older generation could identify. Sponsorship promotion in the video was low-key—celebrities wore Rockport's ProWalker shoes and a family was depicted at the breakfast table eating Total cereal.

In another lifestyle approach to fitness walkers, we positioned General Nutrition Centers (GNC) as "The Home of Fitness Walking." GNC's market research showed that its typical customers are 50 years of age or older, heavy vitamin users, active, upscale socially and economically, and active when it comes to health. This profile matched that of fitness walkers, many of whom were members of mall-walking clubs, that literally walked right past some nine hundred of GNC's stores located in shopping malls.

GNC hired us to develop a detailed, multiphase marketing plan. The plan involved offering a fitness walking kit, which was advertised in several lifestyle publications; a "Fitness Walking Challenge" in which GNC gave away poster maps of the United States and enameled pins each time a walker completed fifteen miles; and a fitness walking sweepstakes providing a trip for four to Hawaii as the grand prize. To position GNC as a leader in the fitness walking field, we arranged for it to sponsor walking clincs featuring fitness expert Gary Yanker and to affiliate with Walkways Center, a nonprofit walking and trails group in Washington, D.C.

SELF-FULFILLMENT AND ENJOYMENT

Most older Americans have reached a point in their lives when self-indulgence is acceptable. They have endured the Great Depression, rationing, and recessions; they have survived several wars; they have sacrificed for their families and children—now they want to enjoy themselves. As *The Mature Americans* survey notes, "They show a strong commitment to spending on products and services that enhance their personal enjoyment of life . . . and many of them now have sufficient discretionary income to act on the new agenda" (Daniel Yankelovich Group, Fall 1987, 7).

As part of that agenda, secure adults are buying luxury items, seeking out life-enhancing experiences, launching post-retirement careers, and finding dream places in which to live.

Cars and clothes head the list of their luxury purchases. The median age of luxury car purchasers is 55 (Schwartz and Stone 1987, 35). For secure adults, luxury cars are a symbol of their well-earned success, prestige, and comfort. And frequently they are driving those luxury cars to clothing stores. A Gallup report revealed that one-third of the women aged 50 and older say they shop for new clothes more often now than when they were in their 30s, and about an equal number (38 percent) of older men also give high priority to buying clothes and accessories (Daniel Yankelovich Group, Fall 1987, 20).

Having purchased most of the "things" they need for survival, most secure adults have shifted their sights to life-enhancing experiences.

HAPPY WANDERERS

It is out of a quest for those vivid experiences that secure adults have become a major market for the pleasure travel and tourism industry. The cruise industry, in particular, benefits, since older Americans account for some 70 percent of all vacationers on cruises (Rosenfeld 1986, 38). Cruises are especially popular with older widows, who see them as a safe, comfortable way to travel. And according to the U.S. Travel Data Center, the 55-plus generation took 220 million domestic trips in 1987, 18 percent of the total of all ages. Nearly one in every eight people over the age of 60 has taken a foreign trip in the past three years and in a year's time, 5 million people 65 and older took a flight, according to studies compiled by United Airlines (Chipkin 1987, 30).

In their travel experiences, secure adults are often as adventurous as the younger generation. They can be found strolling among penguins in Antarctica, riding a train across the Soviet Union, hiking through Europe, participating in Citizen Diplomacy programs, and cruising the Mississippi on a paddle wheeler.

Recognizing the clout of older Americans, nearly every major airline has formed a travel club to attract this age—United Airlines has its Silver Wings Plus; TWA, its Getaway Club 60; and American, its Senior SAAver Club. These clubs offer such incentives as passes, discounts, specially designed tours, and other amenities for the older traveler. And where the airlines go, the hotels, motels, and car rental agencies follow with their own promotions designed to attract the older traveler.

An example of a lifestyle appeal to secure adults with a wanderlust was the co-promotion between Sizzler Restaurants, the popular family restaurant chain, and Delta Airlines. Sizzler advertised a sweepstakes contest open to anyone aged 55 and older. Participants had a chance to win one of ten trips for two to Acapulco or Mexico City on Delta Air Lines. Entry forms for the sweepstakes were brought to Sizzler Restaurants. The back of the entry forms contained promotions on Sizzler's Senior Club food discount program and Delta Air Lines Young-at-Heart program which offered travel discounts.

Even the U.S. government has acknowledged the 55-plus generation's penchant for travel by issuing "Golden Age Passports," which permit anyone aged 60 and older free entry into all national parks and recreational areas. Nearly three-fourths of all the domestic trips taken by older Americans were by car or recreational vehicle (RV) (U.S. Travel Data Center 1989).

Recognizing that large numbers of affluent older Americans own an RV, an executive vice president of a bank came up with a lifestyle marketing program that has worked successfully for more than five years. Valley Bank of Nevada joined forces with the Good Sam Club, the nation's largest RV organization. Most of the club's 580,000 members are older Americans. The product of the bank-club affiliation is the Good Sam Visa card which bears the club logo as well as the usual Visa insignia. The card can be used like any other Visa credit card for the purchase of anything from airline tickets to campground reservations (Friedman 1989).

"An estimated 15,000 Good Sam members have signed up for the card. They receive a 2 percent rebate on any gasoline they charge on the card," explains Peter Friedman, vice president of the bank's consumer finance operations. "The majority of card holders live in Nevada and some have opened checking accounts with us or established other banking relationships. And we haven't begun to explore the other marketing possibilities."

Education

Not only are they traveling for pleasure, but secure adults are also going back to school for fun and self-enhancement, signing up for adult education classes in record numbers. Fueling this growing interest in learning is the rising educational level of the older population during the last several years. In 1970 only about one-fourth of Americans 65 and older had completed high school, now half have; and 10 percent have four or more years of college (AARP 1988, 12). This better-educated population is making learning a life-long avocation. In one U.S. Department of Education study of the 23.3 million people taking one or more adult education courses, 12 percent were 55 years of age or older. In Sarasota County, Florida, half of the students in adult education classes are aged 50 and older (Edmondson, June 1987, 42).

Along with taking classes, secure adults are avid readers, radio listeners, and television watchers, because they have a strong need to be informed about what is happening in their world, nation, and local community. They watch television more than younger age groups, and make up a large share of the audience of news and information programs (Nielsen Media Research 1988, 9-11). They comprise 37 percent of newspaper readers and 33 percent of magazine readers (Berlow 1988).

Recognizing that older readers are a major market, the publishing industry is adding a bevy of new publications—*Second Wind, Family Wealth, Longevity,* and *Lear's*—to such stalwarts as *Modern Maturity* and *50-Plus.*

The banking industry is also discovering that it can penetrate the secure adult market by catering to their interests in both education and travel. Several banks sponsor clubs that present a variety of seminars or take members on day or weekend trips. Usually, the requirement to participate in these programs is a substantial deposit or account balance. One such bank is Bank Five for Savings in Burlington, Massachusetts, which, in November 1986 organized its Presidential Club for customers aged 50 and older.

"We know that the older population is one of the fastest growing markets nationally, and that mature customers are savers and hold high balance deposits," explains Susana Cortez, Presidential Group coordinator, in an interview. "We developed the program to help retain and attract new customers. We address their social and educational needs as well as financial concerns."

To join the Presidential Club, the mature customer must have a minimum $20,000 deposit in any combination of accounts. As a service to the 1,300 club members, Bank Five sponsors cocktail parties, dinner and theater parties, investment seminars, and group trips to Alaska, Hawaii, the Canadian Rockies, and many other sites.

"Many of our club members are widows or married couples seeking to expand their friendship base. The group parties and trips give them a chance to enjoy the company of others," Cortez adds. "Our trips are the number-one club attraction and the social events of the community."

For its efforts, the bank enjoyed retention of many of its valued mature customers and affluent new depositors. An estimated 20 percent of the Presidential Club members are new depositors to the bank (Cortez 1989).

Work—The Second Time Around

Although two-thirds of older workers retire before age 65, many want to continue some kind of part-time work after retirement, and more and more are doing so. Often they work out of a desire to stay active and feel useful rather than a need to earn money. *Modern Maturity*, a bimonthly magazine for the American Association of Retired Persons, polled its readers about second careers. More than 35,000 responded. Among those beyond age 62, only about one-third said they were working primarily for money. One out of five said they were working because they like to work. Surprisingly, most of the respondents also changed occupations—a teacher became a nurse, a nurse became an apple sorter, a Navy officer became a minister, a lawyer became a commercial fisherman.

Tuning into the second career trends, McDonald's has established a McMasters program to teach older Americans how to reenter the labor force through its restaurants. It appealed to the older person who wants to stay involved in life through "New Kid," a sentimental commercial showing an older man going off for his first day of work at a McDonald's (Cain 1988).

Many companies are actively recruiting older workers, including Travelers Corporation of Hartford, Connecticut, and temporary help agencies. Recognizing that money alone will not lure secure adults back into the work force, some companies, such as the *Orange County Register*, employ a lifestyle appeal. In its ad seeking "active seniors" for its new Doorstep Delivery Service, the paper pointed out that "a good walk once a week is: great for your health, great for your outlook and great for your wallet." Faced with a shrinking supply of teenage workers, fast food companies are appealing to the 55-plus generation by offering the flexibility of part-time work.

Making Their Move

Most older Americans do not move away from their hometowns after they retire, but those who do are generally seeking the good life—they want warmth, comfort, and small-town friendship and values. In the last decade, the migration of older Americans across state lines has increased by 50 percent, according to estimates from the Retirement Migration Project. Tired of shoveling snow, slipping on icy streets, and being confined indoors during must of the winter, many of the migrants head for Florida, California, Arizona, and Texas. Together, these states account for nearly half of all the older Americans who move to new states. Other older migrants are fearful of staying in big cities and are heading for the safety and security of places like Heber Springs in Arkansas and Grand Junction in Colorado. And then there are those who claim the best of both worlds. During winter, "snowbirds" increase Florida's population by about 500,000 and Texas' by some 300,000 (Edmondson, November 1987, 27).

Hoping that the snowbirds will nest in their backyards, land developers have urged secure adults to make Florida their "winter retreat" or beckoned them to try out the dry, sunny climate of Arizona by sponsoring low-cost vacations there.

SOCIAL RESPONSIBILITY AND INVOLVEMENT

Blessed with abundant leisure time, secure adults are this nation's hidden resource for volunteers: 83-year-old Clara Hale welcomes AIDS-infected babies to her Hale House; 73-year-old William Rutherford started a nonprofit wildlife preserve in Illinois; 82-year-old Olen Miles and his volunteer helpers have built more than two hundred churches. And they are not alone. Nearly half of those aged 65 to 74 and one-fourth of those 75 and older do volunteer work. Most volunteer "because volunteering gives you a purpose and a place to go. You feel like part of a big family" (*Senior World/Orange County*, June 1986, 4).

The secure adults' involvement in community and church-related volunteer work is a sign of their widely shared "humanistic" sentiment, explains researchers in *The Mature Americans* survey (Daniel Yankelovich Group, Fall 1987, 7). "This 'giving' orientation exists side by side with personal fulfillment needs and does not represent a denial of the self."

Religious organizations are the primary beneficiaries of the secure adults' volunteer efforts, but countless other community groups receive help as well, including the American Cancer Society, the American Heart Association, hospital auxiliaries, political campaigns, musical societies, and even the Peace Corps. The 27-million-member American Association of Retired Persons relies heavily on more than 400,000 volunteers, who help run the organization and participate in lobbying efforts on issues affecting older Americans. The association acknowledges that nearly 35,000 of its members lead driver education classes, provide tax counseling, assist recently widowed men and women in their adjustment to a new life, and help in many other areas of consumer affairs, crime prevention, and housing.

Many secure adults are willing to spend long hours in training to be volunteers. Some take a mandatory eighteen-hour training course from the Literacy Volunteers of America in order to help others learn to read. Peace Corps volunteers spend ten weeks in intensive training before beginning their two years of service abroad.

Recognizing that volunteerism is a vital link to secure adults, several companies run volunteer networks or sponsor special events benefiting local charities. Wells Fargo Bank, for example, had a "Volunteer Network" in California that recruited secure adults to help local nonprofit agencies. A health plan company sponsored a marathon walk for older adults. The entrance fee for the walk was an unwrapped toy which was donated to the Children's Hospital of Los Angeles. Ralphs Grocery Company developed with our help a Ralphs Values Volunteers Program. Community volunteer groups, most of whom were headed by secure adults, nominated members for awards given by Ralphs Grocery. Winners received gift certificates for purchases at Ralphs stores and certificates to hang on their walls. They also had their pictures taken with the local Ralphs store managers. The pictures were posted in the store and published in community newspapers and in newsletters of the volunteer organizations. Not only was the program a success for the volunteers, but it benefited Ralphs as well. The program was honored by then President Ronald Reagan. Many of the volunteer organizations had very large memberships, enabling Ralphs to receive extensive name exposure.

Secure adults also donate large amounts of money to their churches, temples, or favorite charitable organizations. Topping the donor list for all age groups are the 50- to 64-year-olds, who give an average of 3 percent of their income. Close behind them are the 65-plus generation who donates 2.7 percent of their income (Edmondson, November 1986, 46).

Many financial planners have been able to sell an annuity or charitable remainder trust program to older adults by convincing them that these financial products will enable them to leave something to their favority charity, religious organization, college, or cause.

FAMILY ORIENTATION

Because of the cost of living for young families and the increase of single-parent families, secure adults often play a greater role in the lives of their children and grandchildren than they did in the past. Many a divorce-racked family has found both solace and shelter, at least temporarily, with grandparents. Often better off financially than their children, secure adults frequently help their offspring buy their first home, start their own business, or weather a financial crisis.

Not surprisingly, grandchildren are very much a part of the

lives of the 55-plus generation. Secure adults comprise a sub-stantial portion of the toy and children's clothing market, a fact which has not gone unnoticed by the respective industries. Mattel, Inc., introduced its Grandma and Grandpa versions of Ken and Barbie. F.A.O. Schwarz Toy Stores have their own "Grandparents' Boutique" (Dychtwald 1989, 255-56).

The travel industry is also capitalizing on the grandparent connection. Three years ago, Helena Koenig founded Grand-travel, a company which specializes in tours for grandparents and their grandchildren.

"I was a travel agent and grandparent and discovered that there were no programs that addressed the needs of grandpar-ents and grandchildren who wanted to travel together, so I or-ganized Grandtravel," she explains. "In groups of 20, we take children between the ages of 7 and 14 and their grandparents to such places as China, Kenya, England-Scotland, the Ameri-can Southwest, and the Washington, D.C.-Williamsburg, Vir-ginia area. The interest in this kind of travel is very high. I have some 9,000 letters from grandparents who want to go on trips" (Koenig 1989).

As their grandchildren enter the teenage and young adult years, grandparents often help with car purchases or college tuition and expenses. Some investment counselors and colleges are working with secure adults to help them develop financial vehicles to fund their grandchildren's college education.

As these examples illustrate, the trust and business of secure adults is earned by recognizing that they are vital, active, and committed to quality living and by connecting with their inter-ests, attitudes, heroes, and cherished organizations.

WOMEN

The impressive entrance of American women into the work force in the 1970s and 1980s and their emergence as major consumers are among the most profound marketplace transitions of our lifetime.

In just a few decades women's lives have changed dramatically, sending tremors throughout the nation's entire social fabric and economy. The housewife of the 1950s who married early, stayed home, cared for her husband and children, and kept the cookie jar filled with homemade goodies is now a rarity. More than two-thirds (68 percent) of the nation's women with children under 18 now work. A common scenario today is that of a women who rises early, dons a business suit or uniform, quickly feeds her family, bundles up the children, takes them to a baby sitter or day care center, and rushes off to her full-time job. Her paycheck buys essential items for the family or may even support the entire family.

More than half (58 percent) of all women aged 16 and above are working or seeking work, according to *Time* (Wallis December 4, 1989, 82). Yet these aggregate figures mask part of the story. Nearly three-quarters of all women aged 20 to 44 and 69 percent of those aged 45 to 54 are working.

The flow of women into the labor force shows no signs of

slowing. Forecasts indicate that the percentage of women workers will continue to climb. By the year 2000, 61 percent are expected to be working or seeking work, most of them full-time (Johnston and Packer 1987, 85). An in-depth study of American women conducted for *Cosmopolitan* magazine by Battelle Human Affairs Research Centers came to a similar conclusion. The study predicted that women's involvement in the labor force will continue to grow throughout this century and well into the next (Gonzales, March 1988, 19).

As a consequence of their labor force participation, women have acquired formidable economic clout. In 1987, the 55.4 million women aged 16 and older who worked at some time during the year had combined earnings of over $716.6 billion (U.S. Bureau of Labor Statistics, August 3, 1989). Although women have yet to reach financial parity with men, the days of the "59 cent" buttom which symbolized the huge gaps between men and women's wages are waning. Since 1982, according to the U.S. Bureau of the Census, the real earnings for females have outpaced that of their male counterparts (February 1989, 5). A comparison of median weekly earnings for full-time workers in 1988 showed that women earned $315 per ·week while men earned $449, a ratio of 70 cents to every $1 earned by men (U.S. Bureau of Labor Statistics January 1989). Younger women are closing the gap at a faster rate, possibly due to their higher education levels. In 1986, the rate of weekly earnings for full-time women aged 20 to 24 was 86 percent of the earning of males in the same group (McLaughlin and Zimmerle 1988, 7). As their earning power grows, so too, does their influence on this nation's economic well-being.

Their work force participation is not the only propellant moving women to the economic forefront. Another is the rising rate of divorce. Nearly one out of every six families (16 percent) is headed by a female single parent. That statistic represents 10.6 million female heads of households who must make purchase decisions on everything from cantaloupes to cars, paper products to plumbing services, vitamins to videocassette recorders.

BIG-TICKET PURCHASES

In response to these changes, major sectors of our economy that have dealt with male heads of households for generations are having to rethink and revamp their marketing approaches. No longer are cars, stock portfolios, and investment properties "men-only" concerns. Women have become buyers of big-ticket items—automobiles, homes, financial services, travel packages, computers, consumer electronic products, and the like. In 1987, women were the outright purchasers of 45 percent of the new cars sold in the United States, nearly double the amount they bought in 1970, and they influenced 80 percent of all new car purchases, according to studies by J. D. Powers and Associates of Westlake Village, California (Curtindale 1988, 29). This rising number of female purchasers means that the "Good Old Guys" are being sent back to school to learn how to sell cars to women, according to writer Joni Evans (1989, 340). "It isn't easy," Evans comments. "We ask more questions than men, demand more test drives, and look for safety and easy handling over performance and engineering."

More than just the automotive industry is affected by the woman's pocketbook. In the $75-billion-a-year business travel industry, women now comprise 38 percent of all business travelers, up from one percent in 1970 (Cook 1988, 2). Women no longer wait for that "Prince Charming" to come along and buy them that fur coat they have alway wanted. Women are buying their own luxury coats, furriers report, oftentimes more than one, as symbols of their career success (Haynes 1987, 48).

Along with buying big-ticket items, women continue to be the primary decision makers in 80 percent of health care purchases and the majority of grocery purchases, although more and more men and teenage children are being enlisted to help with the family grocery chores.

The needs of working women and dual career families are prompting companies to redirect their approaches and stimulating the growth of many new types of companies and services. There is an increasing number of day care centers, including those which care for babies and sick children. New businesses perform housecleaning and laundry services, catering services, and transportation services for children. To ease the cooking chores of working women, grocery stores have added hot meal takeouts and salad bars, delivery services bring meals from fine restaurants to the home, and microwaveable foods fill the shelves of most freezers.

Whatever the industry, female consumers are likely to be part of the target market. But there are important caveats in marketing to women. One of the major errors corporations make is treating women as a monolithic segment. Certainly, there may be a general sisterhood of women, but within that homogeneous group of 97.6 million females aged 16 and older are marked diversities that must be addressed. In fact, market approaches based solely on women being women often fall flat, as one brokerage firm discovered. The firm opened an office staffed solely by women, thinking that women would prefer to discuss financial issues with other women. The idea failed to bring in the expected female clientele, because the women felt they might be getting different information than men (*Profit Building Strategies for Business Owners* 1988, 11).

Appeals to women should be made on the basis of such lifestyle components as activities, interests, attitudes, and role perceptions. Subsegments to consider include women college students, women working outside the home, women at home, married and single working mothers, women aged 55 years and older, minority women, young women age 16 to 21, women with new families, military women (those in the Armed Forces, civilian employees at military bases, wives of servicemen), and executive or professional women.

Subsegmentation helps a company track its markets more closely, making it easier to forecast the demand for specific types of products or services. The *Cosmopolitan Report* (McLaughlin and Zimmerle 1988), for instance, projects the number of adult women by lifecycle stage and then uses the data to predict future consumption patterns for cars, cosmetics, travel, sportswear, and food. According to the report, the number of women aged 35 to 54 will increase by 15 million between 1985 and 2000, while the number of women aged 34 and under will fall by 5 million. The number of women aged 45 to 54 will grow faster than any other age group, and growth within the segment will be concentrated in the wife and working wife stages.

Subsegmentation also makes it easier to identify the different priorities and activities of women so that marketing approaches can be fine-tuned. *Glamour* magazine found that women's priorities vary significantly with age. For those aged 18 to 24, personal finance was the issue that concerned them most; for women aged 25 to 39, children were most often on their minds; and for women aged 40 to 54, the issue of war and peace was important (Sonenklar 1986, 50). Studies of women aged 18 to 34 who live alone compared to their married or "living together" counterparts found that they went to more movies and plays, traveled outside the United States more often, and read more books—characteristics of obvious interest to the entertainment and travel industries (Russell 1989, 14).

COMMUNICATION PROBLEMS

Many companies fail to communicate intelligently to women. Advertising and marketing approaches often build on stereotypes that many women find offensive, condescending, or guilt-producing. The stereotypes run the gamut—from an inept housewife who cares desperately about water spots on her crystal or the clean smell of her family's clothes and whose happiness depends on her use of products that will solve her problems; to the sex kitten; to the consummate career woman with her stark blue suit and attaché case. And, of course, there is superwoman, whom most women wish would be recalled to Krypton. Ads showing a "superwoman" boasting how she successfully manages a company, her family, and three languages are perceived by most women as unrealistic. Their own experiences tell them otherwise. If they are tired from working eight or nine hours at the office, they will often choose to eat out rather than cook a five-course meal for their families. At a women's forum sponsored by *Ladies Home Journal* (1988, 56), the "superwoman" image was repeatedly attacked.

Beyond the "superwoman" image, women frequently become enraged by ads or approaches that seem to negate their achievements. One underwear manufacturer, for instance, received negative reactions when it ran ads depicting women as doctors and other professionals dressed only in their underwear. Career women protested that the ads reinforced the view of women as sex objects and were demeaning.

In place of stereotypes, women want to be portrayed as mature, intelligent, hard-working decision makers, and as people with a myriad of interests and abilities. More than being portrayed only with sensitivity, women also want to be treated with respect. Countless female customers have been lost because the sales staff have failed to treat them like male consumers. A case in point is one female data processing expert who complains that salespersons in some retail computer stores treat women as computer illiterates. "They think she doesn't know what she wants, has no business tying up that salesperson's valuable time, and therefore can be sold just about anything," writes Frances Mendelsohn (1987, 33).

Even well-meaning attempts to reach women can fail when they are perceived as "separate but not equal." When Hilton Hotels launched its "Lady Hilton" program with designated floors for women, redecorated rooms in pink, and special amenities like perfume in the bathrooms, it was perceived by a majority of women business travelers as condescending (Selinger 1986, 33).

In all types of marketing, it is important to treat women with intelligence, genuineness, respect, and recognition of their achievements. Women are information gatherers and more relationship-oriented than men. Women often seek information and opinions on possible purchases from their peers. They are also avid readers of *Consumer Reports* and do their homework, particularly on major purchase decisions. Usually when they come in the door of a car dealership, electronics store, or computer store, they are ready to buy. In face-to-face sales situations, most women are looking for interaction and cultivation of a relationship and can easily be turned off by the hard sell approach.

If a company is new to marketing to women, it may want to look for alliance relationships with companies that have been reaching this segment for many years—women's magazines, cosmetic companies, and women's clothing stores. Several companies, for example, teamed up with *Mademoiselle* for its in-store events. The magazine brought fashion and beauty shows to upscale department stores around the country. At these events, a New York photographer took pictures of audience volunteers for makeovers to be shown in the magazine; customers asked questions of the publication's fashion and beauty editors; and members of the audience received a bag of gifts from the magazine's advertisers.

REACHING WOMEN

Although an increasingly attractive target market for most companies, women are also becoming harder to reach. In the 1950s and 1960s, household product companies that advertised on daytime soap operas felt confident that they were reaching the majority of their target audiences. Now, with millions of women working, this is no longer true. Compared with traditional homemakers, working women watch 57 percent less daytime television (Steinberg 1988, S-2). When working women come home in the evening, they often face over three hours of child care and housework. They may turn on the television, but also disappear during the commercial breaks to start household tasks.

It is essential to remember that most women today are busy; they do not have time to "chat" about a product. They usually know their purchase decision in advance. To reach them before that purchase decision is made, a company has to capture their attention where they shop, bank, play, socialize, and work, as well as on the way to and from their job.

LIFESTYLE APPROACHES

Women respond well to personalized approaches; one of the most effective ways to reach them is to become involved in the affirmative activities of their lifestyles. Their growing self-identity and independence, their commitment to the labor force and career development, their involvement with childbirth and child rearing, their need for a twenty-six-hour day to handle work, family, and community commitments, their interest in self-improvement and fitness, and their community activism—all offer key lifestyle opportunities upon which to build marketing campaigns.

THE PRIMARY WOMAN

In the 1950s and 1960s, women's lives generally revolved around their family roles and responsibilities. Even purchases they made were based on what they felt their husband and children needed or wanted. They often felt guilty spending on themselves. But the *Cosmopolitan Report* (McLaughlin and Zimmerle 1988, 3, 6) alludes to a fundamental change in the life course of the American woman—the emergence of the "primary woman."

"In the mid-1970s, schooled by the feminism of the 60s, emancipated by the Pill, granted economic independence by the burgeoning job market, a new American woman arrived on the scene: the Primary Woman." The report defines a primary woman as a primary individual in her consumer role, "acting on her own, for her own interest, and with her own buying power."

Articles in women's magazines are no longer on "Understanding Your Husband's Finances" but on "How to Develop Your Own Stock Portfolio," no longer on "How to Make Your Husband Happy," but on "How to Be Your Own Woman." Advertising, too, reflects this shift. In an ad for gold jewelry (*Vogue* 1989, 217), a sophisticated young woman talks about how her mother would be appalled if she bought gold jewelry for herself. In fact, there used to be a lot of things she was not supposed to be able to do for herself—"like earn a good living. And make decisions. All on my own, if I felt like it." The reader has no doubt that this young woman will buy her own gold jewelry.

One of the first companies to tap into the primary woman metality was Philip Morris with its Virginia Slims cigarette cam-

paign in the 1970s. The company began with a new product—
a feminine, slim cigarette. Through its marketing and advertising, it linked its cigarette to the growing self-determination and
career aspirations of the new woman. By sponsoring the Virginia Slims Tennis Circuit, it aligned itself with the equal pay
issues of women and supported Billie Jean King's efforts to increase the earnings of women professional tennis players. L'eggs
followed a similar approach through its sponsorship of the L'eggs
mini-marathon which used the theme "Who Says Women Can't
Run the World" (Folse 1985, 38).

LABOR FORCE COMMITMENT

One of the commonalities among most women today is their
commitment to the labor force. In a "How 40,000 Women Feel
About Their Jobs" survey, *McCall's* magazine found that a wife's
job is no longer considered "extra" money for the family. The
survey participants also said they would return to school or
change jobs to improve their qualifications (Sonenklar 1986, 48).

Along with their labor force commitment, women are moving out of sex-segregated occupations. In the past, women were
generally confined to occupations that were an extension of
mothering—teaching the young, caring for the sick, minister-
ing to the needy. Now, the rigid distinctions between men and
women's work are blurring. Male telephone operators, flight
attendants, and secretaries are no longer an oddity. Women
are becoming lawyers, accountants, physicians, engineers, and
astronauts as well as teachers, nurses, and social workers.
Comparing 1960 with today, the number of female lawyers and
judges has climbed from 7,500 to 180,000, female doctors from
15,672 to 108,200, and female engineers from 7,404 to 174,000
(Wallis, December 4, 1989, 82). Many young women are going
after advanced degrees and entering educational fields once
dominated by men, further breaking down occupational and
wage barriers. Between 1970 and 1988, the proportion of first-
year college coeds planning to earn a doctorate increased from
6.5 percent to 11.4 percent (American Council on Education 1988,
2). According to the U.S. Bureau of Labor Statistics, women

hold approximately 35 percent of the 12.6 million executive, administrative, and management jobs (Battaglia 1989, 64).

Women are also starting their own businesses in record numbers. In 1982, women owned one-fourth of all businesses (excluding corporations), generating some $98.3 billion in gross receipts. Of the 2.9 million women-owned businesses, 92 percent (2.7 million) were individual proprietorships (U.S. Bureau of the Census, April 1986, 2). Four years later, according to special tabulations of the Internal Revenue Service, the number of women-owned sole proprietorships had climbed to 4,121,000. The acceptance of this number of women starting their own businesses is subject to debate. Some observers say it is merely a function of the total number of women entering the work force. Others say it is part of a "cocooning" trend occurring among women who were blocked from moving into upper echelons of corporations, frustrated by inadequate day care for their children, fearful of the burgeoning crime rates in some big cities, and tired of constantly fighting traffic. As a solution to their frustrations, they are starting their own cottage industries, often outfitting their home offices with computers, copies, and facsimile machines.

One of the best ways to join the inner circle of business and professional women is to become partners in their career development and to link with one of some 600 women's business organizations, such as the American Business Women's Association, the National Association of Women Business Owners, Women in Business, Women in Communications, Inc., and the National Association for Female Executives (Wallis December 4, 1989, 89). At the risk of sounding self-serving, it is a good idea to engage the services of a company such as ours to act as an intermediary, because it is important to understand both the corporation's and the professional association's interests and goals and meet both.

Travelers of Farmington, Connecticut, targeted members of the National Association for Female Executives with a direct mail package for automobile and homeowner insurance. The design of the information materials followed the graphic style of all the association's communications (Cleaver 1988, S-10). Atlantic Richfield Company, Litton Industries, and Blue Cross of California were among the corporate patrons of a one-day conference for entrepreneurs, "Nobody's Business But Your Own," sponsored by Women in Communications, Inc. The speakers focused on such issues as discovering niches in the market, managing cash flows, getting new capital, and legal pitfalls. General Motors Corporation's Chevrolet Division sponsored Strategies for Success conferences where it dispensed tips on resumé preparation, stress management, and other career topics. Celebrity speakers for the event included Diahann Carroll and Barbara Walters (Alsop and Abrams 1986, 7). Numerous investment and financial planning companies have successfully run seminars focusing on investment strategies for career women.

MARRIAGE AND FAMILY

Despite their focus on careers, most women deeply value marriage and family life. But there is an important change in the ages at which they are starting their families. Two decades ago, three out of four women started their families before turning 25. Today, women are postponing childbearing, allowing themselves time to get advanced degrees and begin their careers. In 1970, only 14.8 percent of first-time mothers were aged 25 to 29, 3 percent were aged 30 to 34, and only one percent were between 35 and 39. Sixteen years later, more than one-fourth of all women (27.8 percent) waited until they were between 25 and 29 to have their first child, 12.4 percent waited until they were between 30 and 35, and 3.5 percent waited until they were 35 and older (Bonker 1989, J-1). Baby boomers are now having children, creating what has been described as the "boomlet" or "yuppie puppies." Even though the birth rate for these women is much lower than for prior generations, the sheer size of the baby boom generation means that millions of women are new mothers. Baby care, day care, early childhood development, and infant car seat safety have become common concerns. Marketing promotions that address these concerns, perhaps offering partial solutions, may be an effective way to enter this segment's lifestyle.

The health care industry, in particular, has connected with child care concerns. Numerous hospitals have specialized programs for first-time parents, offering monthly newsletters containing information on prenatal and newborn care, counselors to help first-time mothers plan their pregnancy and birth, and celebration dinners for the new parents.

Other companies have connected with child safety concerns, sponsoring child fingerprinting programs and guidebooks for latch-key children. Still others have appealed to the parents' interest in early childhood education and development. Yamaha Music Schools offered music lessons targeted to a 2 1/2- or 3-year-olds and their parents, while a gymnastic center sponsored "Mommy and Me" fitness classes.

With their career, family, social, and community commitments, many women are stressed by conflicting time and energy demands. Women eagerly embrace products and services which can save them time or energy. Convenience (as in catalog shopping, personal shoppers, microwave ovens, all-purpose cleaners) is a high priority in their lives. Companies offering time-saving tips or guidance in easing work-family conflicts are nearly always well received.

THE FITNESS CONNECTION

Despite their dedication to their jobs and families, women believe *they* are important, too, so they attempt to squeeze in time for themselves. Personal appearance and physical fitness are important to most women. An effective way of reaching success-oriented, upwardly mobile women is through athletic and fitness organizations.

Women dominate the aerobics-fitness industry, accounting for 82 percent of the nearly 4 million frequent participants in that sport, according to the National Sporting Goods Association (Doyle 1989, 38). Females also account for 64 percent of the estimated 19.1 million exercise walkers and 59 percent of the estimated 4 million cyclists.

Because of the predominance of women in aerobics, Reebok

saw the sport as a perfect vehicle for reaching women. It set out to make the Reebok name synonymous with the beginning of the aerobics movement. The company developed an aerobics shoe based upon advice from aerobic instructors.

"Our shoe was the first one designed specifically for aerobics from the bottom up," says Angel Martinez, vice president of business development. "It was the only product at the time offering instructors the feel, fit, and cushion they wanted."

Reebok did not stop with shoe design. It sponsored the first certification program for aerobics instructors, established the Reebok instructor alliance program, published aerobics newsletters, made its products available to instructors at professional prices, sponsored aerobics seminars, co-sponsored national aerobics championships, ran ads in fitness publications, and organized a clearinghouse for information about injury prevention (Martinez 1988, 16).

As a result of the company's involvement in aerobics, sales of Reebok athletic shoes sprinted ahead, reaching more than $1 billion in recent years. Equally as important for ongoing market share, Reebok shoes became symbols of the affluent, active, success-oriented lifestyle. Executive women wear them to and from the office; young professionals wear them when they go shopping; working mothers wear them when they take their children to the park or zoo. Many of their children wear Weeboks, illustrating the principle that if a mother trusts the shoes for herself, she will also buy them for her family.

The Reebok lesson has been learned well by other companies that are targeting the active women's market by relying on the fitness connection. A foreign car manufacturer that has designed a stylish, popularly priced car targeted toward active lifestyle women developed alliances with fitness organizations. The company maintained a presence at fitness conferences, participated in awards presentations and recognition dinners for leaders in the field, and linked up with causes dear to the hearts of fitness instructors. It sponsored a Drive Away Heart Disease promotion in which it made a donation to heart disease research for each test drive taken by participants of the campaign.

COMMUNITY ACTIVISM

As they become parents, many women become increasingly concerned about and involved with civic and religious organizations, nonprofit groups, and causes. Even if time is limited, women will help in specific ways.

Armed with this knowledge, Scott Paper Company launched its Helping Hands program in 1986 to appeal to female heads of households (Deitrich 1989).

"We know that women are heavy purchasers of packaged goods and are also very interested in causes related to children," explains Don Deitrich, unit director for Helping Hands, in an interview. "Our goals in launching the project were to improve our volume of earnings, improve the company's image among its key customers, and do something socially responsible."

In three years, the Helping Hands project raised an estimated $3 million for charities helping children with special needs, such as Easter Seals, March of Dimes, and the Cystic Fibrosis Foundation. The company, Deitrich explains, carefully selected the charities, looking at the strength of their volunteer base, the quality and reputation of their programs, and the soundness of their financial and administrative operations.

Other companies have also linked their products to programs supporting children as a way of reaching the female consumer. Campbell Soup Company used a soup label redemption program to help schools buy needed equipment, and Procter & Gamble Company employed a coupon redemption program for Special Olympics.

As they reach middle age and beyond, many women devote increasingly more time to civic organizations and causes. These activists are frequently better educated, more informed, and more affluent than the average woman. They are likely to be attractive prospects for a company, particularly because they are key influencers of other women.

To tie into these community activists, the Working Assets Fund Service in San Francisco established a special Visa card program. Each time a Visa card was used, the company made donations to women's foundations across the country that allocated funds to worthwhile causes (Gonzales, January 1988, 23).

Tapping the women's segment may be one of the most challenging tasks undertaken by a company, but the segment is far too important to ignore. Billions of dollars in buying power await companies which recognize that women are a major independent economic force and align with them.

COLLEGE STUDENTS

Despite appearances, college students buy much more than music tapes, posters, and jeans. No segment of the marketplace holds more potential for the action-oriented marketer.

Today's college students are tomorrow's most affluent consumers, earning over $600,000 more than their high school graduate counterparts over their lifespan(Finn 1988, 24). And this disparity escalates as the number of years of college education increases. Families headed by high school graduates, according to the U.S. Bureau of the Census (February 1989, 4), had annual median incomes of $29,937 in 1987 while families headed by those with four or more years of college had annual incomes of $46,533 and those with five or more years of college education had $54,491.

The best time to approach these future high earners is even before they enter college. Many students buy cars in their senior year of high school or during the summer before they enter college. Once they reach college, these young people set up mini-households; they buy groceries; they pay utility bills; they do their first serious banking; they buy cars, clothing, and sporting goods; they travel and take vacations. "This is the time of life where they're willing to try new products, when they form habits and brand loyalties," says John Haring, senior marketing manager with Campbell Soup Company. "This is the time to get them in your franchise" (Weinstein 1988, S-6).

College students are also America's most important trend setters, influencing not only siblings and high school students, but their parents and society as a whole. While the cost of reaching them may be higher, college students have a disproportionate influence on others and on the communities in which they live.

AN ACTIVE MARKET

College students spend between $20 and $45 billion annually on discretionary purchases (College Stores Research and Educational Foundation 1986, 1; Graham and Hamden 1987). In a national survey conducted by the College Stores Research and Educational Foundation, students were asked how much money they had available to spend each month on nonschool-related expenditures. Three out of five had $100 or more per month to spend, and of those one in eleven (8.8 percent) had more than $450. Much of their discretionary income comes from their own labor—about 92 percent of them hold part- or full-time jobs (Simmons Market Research Bureau, Inc. 1985). And when their cash reserves become low, more than half of them can pull out their Master, Visa, or American Express card and charge it (College Stores Research and Educational Foundation 1986, 5). Beyond their own resources, students can often call upon their parents or grandparents for help, particularly when buying a car, computer, or other major items. This phenomemon, called "extended dependency," is a system where parents add enough money to their son's or daughter's income for a safe environment and a comfortable standard of living.

Where do those discretionary dollars go? Clothing, toiletries, and cosmetics account for the highest percentage of dollars spent. Some 96 percent of students in a nationwide survey said they spent more money on clothes during a year than on any other item. Often, those clothes were high fashion rather than jeans. Additionally, more than half of the students (62 percent) bought cars, trucks, or vans, of which 19 percent were purchased new;

95 percent bought snack foods; 88 percent bought records and tapes; and 71 percent bought cameras and film (College Stores Research and Educational Foundation 1986, 5). Some of their expenditures were for high-tech products, including computer equipment and supplies and portable electronic typewriters.

CHANGES ON CAMPUSES

Dramatic changes have occurred on college campuses, both in the size and composition of the student body. In 1970, there were some 8.6 million college students; today there are 12.5 million, a market equal to the population of Southern California. Despite the trumpeted baby bust, this level of enrollment is expected to remain relatively stable until a rise in the late 1990s. More and more high school graduates are opting for college and older adults are returning to school.

The typical college student was once a recent high school graduate who lived on campus and obtained a degree in four years. Today less than half the students earn their degrees in the traditional four years, according to the National Center for Educational Statistics. Increasingly, middle-aged adults are found among recent high school graduates. Of the more than twelve million college students, more than 39 percent are aged 25 and older and 14.5 percent are aged 35 and older. Many of these older students are returning to college to complete their education or are college graduates who are changing careers. Most are married and three out of four have jobs (U.S. Bureau of the Census, August 1988, 18, 63).

Once primarily male bastions, college campuses are attracting more and more women. In fact, women are now in the majority. In 1972, there were 3.9 million female students enrolled in U.S. colleges and universities, 42 percent of that year's total. Today, women students number 6.7 million and constitute 53 percent of the total (Finn 1988, 24). And not only are there more female undergraduates than males, but more women are heading for advanced degrees and professional schools of business, law, medicine, and engineering. In the annual American Council on Education/UCLA survey of entering college freshmen, the proportion of freshmen women planning to earn a doctorate increased by two-thirds between 1970 and 1988, from 6.5 to 11.4 percent (1988, 2).

Sizable numbers of minority students attend college, particularly Asian Americans. Some 2.25 million minority students are enrolled in American colleges and universities (Finn 1988, 24).

COMMUNITY COLLEGES

Perhaps because they lack the football visibility of major league schools and the prestige of the private Ivy League universities, two-year community colleges are often ignored by corporate America. Yet these community colleges—particularly in California, Texas, Washington, Florida, Illinois, and New York— are the real "sleepers" in the area of college marketing opportunities. About one-third of all American undergraduate students attend two-year colleges. California's community colleges enroll an estimated 1.1 million students, about one out of every 11 college students in the United States (*Chronicle of Higher Education* 1988).

Enrollment at community colleges is steadily rising. This is partly due to the admission's squeeze at major state-supported universities. The universities are recommending that applicants complete their first two years at a junior college. Other students are obtaining two-year specialized training as nurses, computer operators, court reporters, paramedics, police, and firemen. But not all community college students are career-focused. Large numbers of the general population, particularly those aged 50 and older, are enrolling in self-enrichment, small business, and leisure activities offered at nearby community colleges. Because of the diversity of the student body and the high numbers, community colleges are perfect for tie-ins with local businesses, such as car dealerships and community banks.

Although students at community and other colleges are obvious marketing targets, there is a hidden element to the college market—the greater college community. This community includes professors, administrators, physicians and nurses on staff at teaching hospitals and research centers, security personnel, concerned parents, alumni, and people in the community who attend special events at colleges. It also encompasses the community surrounding the college—the fast food restaurants, sports and recreational facilities, independent bookstores, movie theaters, and pubs—frequented by the students. College marketing must have a broad perspective. A company could do a college marketing program that goes beyond the college bookstore and reaches into the greater college community. Beer companies, for example, may not find themselves welcome on many college campuses, but they can still reach college students through marketing programs at pubs and restaurants surrounding the campus.

ENTERING THE COLLEGE MARKET

Before launching a college marketing program, a company needs to consider some particularities. Most importantly, a company must not expect colleges to operate with the same time frame as the business community.

"Colleges do not modify their schedules to meet corporate fiscal years and budgets," warns Gerald Fecht, a marketing professor. "If your objectives are to impact the student community, you have to consider that the college lifestyle holds the summer sacred, takes two weeks off at Christmas, a week off at Easter, vanishes during the quarter or semester breaks and sees the year beginning in August or September and ending in May or June. College administrators establish budgets and set school schedules just before summer which means you should have your programs developed for their review by April or May." (Fecht 1989)

The increasing sophistication of students also poses a special challenge. Today's college students have been saturated with multimedia advertising approaches and are more discerning than their predecessors. With most of them working, they are also more experienced in spending their money. This is not to say that college students are totally unapproachable, but neither are they an easy mark. What they do respond to is originality and quality.

Because of the dynamic nature of the college market, a company needs to maintain an ongoing presence on campus. Remaining in the marketplace permits a company to monitor the changing values and interests of college students. It also enables it to address the problem of a high turnover rate (graduates). A company may reach students this year, but by next year more than one-third of them will be different. To promote top-of-mind awareness, a company's image and message must constantly be reinforced.

Perhaps the most perplexing factor in college marketing is the increase in "media clutter." Once the almost exclusive domain of beer companies, U.S. college campuses have become a high-priority market target for a number of businesses, including automotive companies, the financial services industry, computer manufacturers, fast food suppliers, cosmetic companies, clothing manufacturers and retailers, and soft drink beverage companies. With this proliferation of businesses has come an increase in the number of media and promotional vehicles needed to reach them. The challenge is how to choose among them and not fritter away precious marketing dollars with nothing to show for them.

For a generation raised in front of the television, it would seem that this is a natural way of reaching college students. But the truth is that it is tough to target students through conventional media. College students are erratic television watchers, tuning in for about 21.8 hours of television a week (Vakil 1989, S-8), much less than the 49.5 hours for the general population. When they do turn on their sets, their preferences range from "Late Night with David Letterman" to "Days of Our Lives." But there are also some very real questions about the quality of the students' attention to television shows, since many study or socialize while the set is turned on. Listening to the radio is less common than watching television. In a 1988 study, Simmons Market Research Bureau found that two-thirds listened to less than two hours of radio each day (*Advertising Age* 1989, S-10).

Given that college students are difficult to reach via traditional media, companies are exploring the use of campus magazines, sampling campaigns, cable television programs, music videos, on-campus cinema advertising, wall media, publication of official class directories, direct mail, spring break promotions, on-campus newspapers and radio, on-campus promotions, kiosks, and a plethora of other approaches.

In the last five years or so, the number of campus magazines has tripled. Some of these magazines were backed by such publishing heavyweights as *Businessweek*, *Newsweek*, and *Time*. But this large number of magazines—thirty-eight at one time in 1988—led to an inevitable shakeout. Several magazines failed to attract national advertisers because of poor distribution (many were drop-distributed) and the lack of credible readership documentation; some of the touted pass-along rates for campus magazines are well beyond reasonable estimates. To determine how much college-directed magazines are read, *Advertising Age* polled marketing communications and journalism students at twelve colleges across the country and found that 48 percent read campus magazines (Sherer 1989, S-10). But the tough questions here are which ones to what extent? A better bet for a print campaign incorporating quality color graphics is *U, the National College Newspaper*. A color tabloid, *U* contains a compilation of articles, editorials, and photographs from college newspapers around the country. It is frequently distributed as a supplement within a college newspaper.

Similar to college magazines, the campus-direct electronic media has also proliferated, with players including the National College Television and MTV. As with traditional television, there is still the question of how much time students actually spend watching the programs.

With so many companies wanting to get their personal care, food, and other products in the hands of students before their buying loyalties are formed, sampling campaigns have become an increasingly popular marketing tool. Commenting on the value of sampling, *Advertising Age* writer Janice Steinberg says asking if college students are good subjects for sampling is like asking if the pope is Catholic (February 1, 1988, S-28). Most campus sampling programs involve co-op packs containing a variety of sampler products ranging from toiletries to coupons for film development. They are distributed in dorm rooms, bookstores, at graduation, at concerts, even in hotels gearing up for the annual onslaught of students during spring break. About 29.3 percent of the respondents in the *Advertising Age* polls said they have responded to samples (Sherer 1989, S-10). Trackers of the results of sample packs say they do increase top-of-mind awareness and sales. Drawbacks include abuse by students and lack of product exclusivity in co-op programs.

Some of the newer innovations for reaching college students include wall boards and electronic bulletin boards. Wall boards are usually posters containing magazine-style features and one or two ads hung in wall-mounted display cases in student unions and other high-traffic campus locations. Electronic bulletin boards with circulating messages are usually placed in college cafeterias and other gathering places for students. While these may be effective marketing approaches, there is some difficulty in quantifying the number of impressions.

From our experiences in college marketing, we have found campus newspapers and lifestyle events on campus to be among the most effective ways to reach this illusive but lucrative market. Advertising in a college newspaper is an excellent investment, both from a readership and cost per impression perspective. With articles about campus events, personalities, and issues, college newspapers are about the only print media students read on a regular basis. An estimated 85.2 percent of full-time undergraduates and 70.7 percent of the total student body read college newspapers at least one time per week, according to a Simmons Marketing Research Bureau survey (*Advertising Age* 1989, S-10).

In its own survey of 1,200 students at twenty-four schools, American Telephone and Telegraph (AT&T) found that students remember its ads in campus newspapers much more than ones in campus-directed magazines, wall boards, and other media (Steinberg 1989, S-4). Along with AT&T, other major corporations have developed confidence in college newspapers. Zenith Data Systems began advertising its portable computers in campus papers, calling attention to its truckload sales. Miller Brewing Company uses college newspapers to advertise special off-campus events like the Miller Lite Ski Festival and spring break activities. We work frequently with college newspapers in placing ads for General Motors Corporation and other clients. When working with a college newspaper, it helps to be patient, flexible, and tolerant. Each college newspaper has it own advertising policy which necessitates flexibility on the part of any corporate advertiser. Moreover, campus newspapers are primarily educational tools for journalism schools, so the advertising may be less than perfect and the stories covered may be less professional than in the *Los Angeles Times*.

LIFESTYLE APPROACHES

Success in college marketing comes from tracking student attitudes, goals, and values; playing an active role in the students' positive lifestyle activities; and playing according to a specific college's rules. This is accomplished by working cooperatively with college deans, faculty, and student representatives on an ongoing basis; by regularly reading college newspapers; and by never leaving the college market.

STUDENT ATTITUDES

One of the biggest misconceptions about today's college students is that they display the same concern for political and social causes as the generation of the 1960s and 1970s. A few in-depth conversations with today's college students will dispel that perception. If the conversations are not convincing enough, the differences are documented in a report, *The American Freshman, Twenty Year Trends: 1966-1985*, which is based on annual surveys of some 280,000 college freshmen at 550 two- and four-year colleges. Perhaps because of the upheavals in our economy over the last decade and the recognition that it is increasingly difficult for single-income families to make ends meet, today's freshmen are concerned most about money and being well off financially. Other values high on their list include power, status, being an authority, having administrative responsibility for others, and obtaining recognition. Compared to the 1960s and 1970s generations, today's college students are less zealous about helping others, promoting racial understanding, cleaning up the environment, participating in community action programs, and keeping up with political affairs (American Council on Education 1986, 2). A 1988 survey of college freshman found a continuance of materialistic values. A record 76.7 percent of the freshmen indicated that making more money was a very important factor in their decision to attend college, up from 49.9 percent in 1971. Some 73.4 percent indicated that being well off financially was a major life objective, nearly double the level reached in 1970 (American Council on Education 1988, 60).

Campaigns that tap into students' focus on economic security and status, therefore, are more likely to be successful. AT&T, for example, has a Collegiate Investment Challenge, a game that simulates Wall Street trading. Students attempt to win more than $200,000 in cash and prizes by building portfolios (Steinberg 1989, S-4). Recognizing that for a student, owning a credit card is a status symbol, BankAmericard, American Express, and City Bank have actively courted college students. Students who meet specific requirements receive automatic approval; representatives come to campuses to help students fill out applications during the back-to-school months.

Linked with the concern for financial security and prestige is a desire to find a financially rewarding career. Some advertisers are placing print ads in niche magazines which focus on careers and are distributed through career placement offices. The *Wall Street Journal* demonstrates that it understands student concerns with its "How to Get a Job" guidelines distributed on campuses across the country. Similarly, Honda has placed job hunting guidebooks into students' hands. Other corporations reach students by sponsoring job fairs and career days.

Most of the "rewarding" careers sought by today's students require a college diploma as a prerequisite. And that diploma costs money. In 1983, the average cost of a bachelor's degree was $24,700. Today, it is estimated at $36,800 (Finn 1988, 24). To help pay the costs, students rely on a number of resources, including financial assistance from family members, guaranteed student loans, scholarships, earnings from jobs, and stipends from employers.

Understanding the financial crunch confronting most students, several major corporations are linking their product promotions to scholarship awards. Campbell Soup Company's Chunky Soup Division came up with a $5,000 sweepstakes called "Chunky takes a bite out of your tuition" (Steinberg 1989, S-4). As part of its National Collegiate Alcohol Awareness Week, Adolph Coors Company gave a scholarship award of $1,000 to winning campuses. To honor students who have contributed to the betterment of their schools and communities, General Motors provided Spirit Awards at campuses across the country. Winners received certificates and shares of GM common, GM-Hughes, and GM Electronic Data Systems stock. Soft drink beverage companies have launched a variety of college scholarship programs for minority students.

Nearly all college students express an interest in the future. To a great extent, this is self-evident, since most students are on campus to prepare for their futures. They are curious about what their lives will be like in ten or twenty years and are fascinated by the impact of lasers, satellites, robots, computers, and other technological innovations. To capitalize on this interest, a company might co-sponsor a Future Expo which would showcase current high-tech products and feature presentations by top scientists, science fiction writers, and futurists, forecasting trends in science, health, business, industry, agriculture, jobs and education, the political scene, and society in general.

COMMUTERS

Today nearly half of all college students live off campus and are commuters. Among two-year college students, the number of commuters climbs to some 95 percent. Obviously, the techniques that work at Rutgers State University of New Jersey or Brown University with their high residential populations may be less effective with students attending California State University at Northridge, the University of Texas at Arlington, or other commuter schools.

Commuter students are a particularly attractive market for automobile manufacturers, dealers, or suppliers. Over one million students alone commute to California's community colleges. Commuter students can occasionally be reached through radio advertising. But there are alternatives. The University of Southern California, for example, has its own *Parking Lot Press* aimed at commuter students which contains discount coupons for fast foods and other products. Another possible approach might be a commuter sampler kit with free coupons for coffee and donuts, hide-a-key containers, and sweepstake entry forms for a new car.

Some of the most effective ways to reach commuter and residential students alike are through special events and college organizations—particularly intramural athletic clubs, religious organizations, fraternities or sororities, and special interest groups. Every campus is different, however, and a company must pick which organizations and events it is going to support. At the University of California at Los Angeles, for example, a key event is the Mardi Gras Carnival which helps fund Unicamp, UCLA's official charity. Unicamp is for Los Angeles children who might otherwise not have a residential camping experience. At Cornell University, ice sculpture contests are popular.

RECREATIONAL SPORTS

Common denominators that bridge across campuses are college recreational sports, especially intramurals.

Although intramural sports are not part of physical education classes or intercollegiate competitions, more than one-fourth (27.9 percent) of students of both sexes as well as college staff and faculty participate in them. Such sports may include organized competitive or drop-in play, sports clubs, clinics, special events, and outdoor recreation. Sponsorship of intramurals generally works and is a major link to students. At the University of California at Santa Barbara alone, for instance, there are some eight hundred volleyball teams. Seeing an opportunity, a major car manufacturer sponsored a Volleyball Classic there. General Motors Corporation has a marketing alliance with several campuses and has sponsored numerous Intramural Campus Fests. Domino's Pizza tied in with recreational sports through sponsorship of team tennis leagues. For the most part the leagues are preexistent intramural, fraternity, or club programs. Besides providing drawsheets, posters, and recruiting materials, Domino's also gave T-shirts, visors, and towels to participating players. Each member of a winning team got an additional award as well.

Beer companies in particular have added some creative twists to campus sports sponsorships. Coors sponsored a New Games Development program involving giant beach ball and parachute events. Budweiser ran inserts for college newspapers—"Spuds MacKenzie presents the athlete of the month"—while Miller ran inserts in college papers congratulating intramural champions.

When contemplating the sponsorship of a campus sports program, a company must be prepared to allocate about three times the cost of the sponsorship for promotion. A company needs to publicize its sponsorship to produce the desired exposure and results.

These sponsorships do pay off. Sievers Research asked a number of students if they could recall the name of any companies or corporations that are either presently or have in the past been involved with or sponsored events or activities on campus. The students identified those companies which have traditionally utilized intramural/recreational sports to reach the total college community.

One of the reasons recreational sports sponsorship works well is the type of students attracted to sports competitions. Generally, they look fit and healthy, they are friendly and outgoing, and they are among the best-looking people on campus. They influence other students.

"THE GREEKS"

Just as fraternities and sororities are rushing students, a company can rush the Greek letter organizations. One out of six (17.8 percent) college students are affiliated with fraternities and sororities, and the numbers are growing. In a 1988 *College Store Journal* article, writer Veronica Hughes reports there are some 400,000 fraternity men and some 225,000 sorority women.

Among the reasons students give for joining such organizations are that it looks good on their resumé; it will help in their careers; it will provide them with instant status, reputation, and identification; and it will allow them to make powerful and important social connections.

The Greeks have influence far beyond their numbers. These students are often "movers" and "shakers" who are involved in campus political organizations and community and campus betterment projects; and they usually have more discretionary income due to higher family incomes. Because they are easily reached through the structure of the fraternity or sorority house, these students are ideal for sampling programs. General Foods Corporation, for example, used the sorority connection to launch a sampling program for its International Coffees. More than two hundred thousand samples, one for each sorority member, were sent to sororities on some one thousand campuses (Steinberg, February 1, 1988, S-28).

THE RITE OF SPRING

Each spring, thousands of students beseige such places as Daytona Beach, Florida, and Palm Springs, California, seeking a respite from the stress of studies, term papers, exams, and parental expectations. They gather to have fun, socialize, and party.

The number of spring break participants, reaching near four hundred thousand in Daytona, for instance, merit attention by any business suitor of the college market. Some of the biggest companies in the nation try to outdo each other to show students a good time. They shower them with T-shirts, mugs, and nonstop entertainment. So much so that clutter has become a serious concern. Symptomatic of this clutter is Daytona Beach, where Playboy-Ujena Swimwear had a bikini contest, Caribe sponsored a wet T-shirt contest, and Budweiser held a best male body contest. All along the beach, myriads of volleyball competitions were sponsored by Pontiac, Diet Pepsi, Coppertone, Coors Light, and Plymouth (Lipman 1989, B-1).

To stand out from the clutter at spring break events requires ingenuity and creativity. One such ingenious approach involved teams of college women dressed in tuxedos, who went door-to-door in the major beachfront hotels offering to spray men with samples of Pierre Cardin men's cologne. Timing of the sampling was propitious. It occurred in the late afternoon, reaching the male students just as they were getting ready to go out for the evening (Steinberg, February 1, 1988, S-27).

TRAVEL

Traveling to nearby resorts for spring break activities is by no means the only traveling students do. Many use their summer vacations to travel to Europe, Mexico, and other attractive locales. In one survey, more than one-fourth (26 percent) of the students said they travel abroad (College Stores Research and Educational Foundation 1986, 5). Travel tie-ins are one way to lure students to sample a company's products. For instance, General Foods offered free tasting of its Suisse Mocha coffee in 135 college bookstores along with a sweepstakes promotion offering a trip to Switzerland (Sherrid and Lanier 1986, 45).

MUSIC AND MOVIES

Several major corporations have used music in innovative ways to attract college students. Chevrolet sponsored video dance parties which provided three hours of videos by such recording artists as Billy Joel and Bruce Springsteen. Half the proceeds from the events went to a cancer research foundation and the rest to campus organizations. Commercials for Chevy cars and trucks ran during the videos (Serafin 1987, S-14). American Express vied for student loyalty by sponsoring "Star Bound" talent shows; one talent show at the University of Miami drew twenty thousand people. TDK Electronics Corporation set up a recording booth at the Daytona spring break festivities, where students could get a free TDK tape of themselves singing their favorite songs backed up by instruments. The promotion was a natural draw, since college students saw their peers performing right in front of them (Steinberg, February 1988, S-26).

While music is in the main interest in the college student's entertainment scenario, movies also continue to play a major role. For that reason, some corporations sponsor on-campus film fests while others, including Columbia Pictures and Twentieth Century Fox, go for high visibility among spring break revelers.

While the vehicle may be movies, music, or intramural sports, these lifestyle approaches enable companies to go beyond advertising to penetrate the emotional centers of students. It is from these centers that favorable attitude shifts, purchase consideration, and long-term loyalties are fostered.

HISPANICS

The names of Anheuser-Busch, Inc., American Telephone & Telegraph Company, and Coca-Cola USA are now commonplace on the sponsorship list for Carnaval Miami, a popular Hispanic festival. In Los Angeles, Philip Morris Companies, Inc., and Anheuser-Busch, Inc., are among the sponsors of Plaza de la Raza, a nonprofit group that presents musical concerts and art exhibits for the Hispanic community.

For years American businesses have been urged to pay attention to this segment. Today, more and more are listening. We went through the conversion process ourselves while handling licensing and merchandizing arrangements for the City of Los Angeles' Bicentennial Celebration in 1981. The size of the city's Hispanic population (27 percent) surprised us. This was a major, virtually untapped market. Convinced of the breadth and potential of this Hispanic segment, we presented our research of Ford Motor Company and Ralphs Grocery Company and took their top management on tours of the Hispanic communities of Los Angeles. Both these companies became pioneers in Hispanic marketing.

"We recognized the growth potential and vitality of the Hispanic market in Southern California, and decided to target it in a pre-emptive way," explains Alfred Marasca, Ralphs' executive vice president of marketing. "We added food products that would appeal to Mexican-Americans and other Hispanics, we hired local Spanish-speaking employees, and we began building ties with key organizations in the Hispanic communities through sponsorship of special events. Our goal is to make Hispanics feel they are valued not just as customers, but as people" (Marasca 1989).

A GROWING MARKET

From 1980 to 1988, the Hispanic population has increased by 34 percent, four times the overall U.S. population growth. The United States is already the sixth largest Hispanic-populated country in the world (Strategy Research Corp. 1986, 38). And by the year 2000, Hispanics are expected to comprise 10 percent of the U.S. population, increasing from the current 19.4 million to an estimated 31.2 million.

The rate of these increases shows no sign of abating. The high birth rate among Hispanic women and the constant flow of new immigrants will continue to fuel this population explosion. Both married and unmarried Hispanic women are having more children earlier in life than non-Hispanic women. Even when data are controlled for education level, professional status, and personal income, Hispanic women have more children than their non-Latino counterparts (Arce 1987, 5).

The immigration flow is also expected to continue. More than one-third of the immigrants to the United States in the 1980s came from Latin America and Spain. Some were political refugees from Cuba, Nicaragua, Guatemala, and El Salvadar, while others fled the financial uncertainties of Mexico and other Latin countries whose economies have been crippled by the debt crisis. Hispanics come to the United States because "they need dollars. They need food. Maybe they need to get out of the way of bullets," says author Richard Rodriguez (1988, 84). Certainly, in their search for a better life and more opportunities, the Hispanic immigrants are no different from the waves of European immigrants who preceded them.

POPULATION REVERBERATIONS

With our corporate offices in Los Angeles County, we have watched this "county of the angels" evolve into one of the world's largest urban Spanish-speaking communities. Nearly one-third of the population here is of Hispanic origin. The impact is obvious. Walk through East Los Angeles and it is like walking through Mexican cities. There are Mexican cafes, panaderías (bakeries), outdoor murals, news racks stuffed with *La Opinion* newspapers, Latin music emanating from portable tape players, parks filled with Mexican families and friends enjoying a barbecue or picnic, and animated conversations in Spanish everywhere.

Los Angeles County is a place to gain a grass-roots foothold in the U.S. Hispanic market, not only because of the magnitude of the Hispanic population, but also because of its impact on Latinos in other U.S. cities in terms of attitudes, fashions, and lifestyles. Just as Hollywood and Southern California are trendsetters for the general population, so too, is Los Angeles County for the U.S. Hispanic population.

While Los Angeles is perhaps the top Hispanic market, several other states and metropolitan areas have significant concentrations. From a marketing perspective, this is a plus, since these clusters are easily indentifiable and accessible. Fifty-five percent of all Latinos in the nation reside in California and Texas. California's 6.6 million Hispanics generally are clustered in cities originally settled by early Franciscan friars and bearing such spanish names as Los Angeles, San Francisco, San Diego, Santa Ana, San Jose, and Santa Barbara. Because of the state's proximity to Mexico, most Hispanics are of Mexican origin or descent, although there are Guatemalans, Salvadorans, Nicaraguans, South Americans, and Cubans sprinkled among them.

The automotive and food products industries cannot afford to ignore the Hispanic market in the Southwest. Texas is home of 4.1 million Hispanics, most of whose families originally came from Mexico. Large Hispanic communities can be found in the San Antonio, Houston, the Dallas-Fort Worth area, and the border cities of El Paso, Laredo, McAllen, and Brownsville. In

San Antonio, in particular, a company can take the pulse of the nation's Mexican-American subsegment. It is the fourth ranked Hispanic market in the country and nearly 50 percent of the population in the San Antonio area is Hispanic. San Antonio residents love and are proud of their city. It has a rich Hispanic culture and heritage, and many of the community and government leaders are of Mexican descent. In other areas of the Southwest, New Mexico and Arizona each have more than one-half million Hispanics and Colorado has 368,000. By the way, I believe that if a company targets the Southwest, California, or Los Angeles as a major or trend-setting market, it will never win the market unless it considers the Hispanic segment.

Hispanics have also become a significant consumer segment in the Northwest, South, and Midwest. New York and New Jersey are home to millions of Hispanics, most of whom are Puerto Rican, although there are also clusters of Cubans, Mexicans, Dominicans, and South and Central Americans. The majority of New York's 2.1 million Hispanics live in the five boroughs of New York City, while New Jersey's 646,000 Hispanics make their homes in Bergen-Passaic, Newark, Hackensack, and Hoboken. Other urban pockets of Hispanics exist along the Atlantic seaboard, including Hartford, Connecticut, and Philadelphia, Pennsylvania.

With its own "Little Havana," Florida is home to 1.5 million Hispanics. Cubans, along with some South and Central Americans, are not only leaving their imprint on Miami but also on Tampa and St. Petersburg. Generally, Cubans who emigrated to the United States during the 1960s had a head start over other Hispanic immigrant groups. Many were middle- or upper-class professionals and business leaders who brought their skills with them. Educated and usually bilingual, they moved into the business life of Florida. Some joined mainstream American corporations while others became entrepreneurs, establishing banks, real estate companies, import and export firms, and other businesses.

In the Midwest, some 801,000 Hispanics live in Chicago. What is intriguing about Chicago is that it is a near microcosm of the national Hispanic population with a mix of Mexicans, Puerto Ricans, Cubans, and South and Central Americans.

PURCHASING POWER

Hispanics, in general, can afford and are willing to spend much more than companies realize. The annual total money income for Hispanics above the age of 15 was $147.9 billion for 1987, according to U.S. Bureau of the Census reports (February 1989, 122). Even higher estimates come from Strategy Research Corp., which placed U.S. Hispanic buying power at $171.1 billion in its *1989 U.S. Hispanic Market Study* (Strategy Research Corp. 1989, 5).

Despite the stereotypes of poverty-striken Hispanics, there is a substantial and growing Hispanic middle class. One out of every four Hispanic families has an income in excess of $35,000 (U. S. Bureau of the Census, August 1988(A), 15). There is a growing number of Hispanics in professional and managerial positions. Between 1984 and 1988, the number of Hispanic women working as managers and professionals rose from 12.8 to 15.7 percent, while the number of Hispanic men working as managers and professionals increased from 11.5 to 13 percent (U.S. Bureau of the Census, August 1988(B), 11).

Although Hispanic families have lower annual median incomes compared to the general population not of Hispanic origin ($20,306 vs. $31,610), much of that disparity can be traced to recent immigrants. After living in this country ten or more years, the family incomes of Hispanics tend to equal or exceed that of their non-Hispanic counterparts (Lopez 1987, 11). No matter what their income levels, Hispanics strive to do well by their families, and they spend more of their disposable income on groceries, appliances, cars, and trucks. It is important to recognize, also, that young Latinos often are major contributors to their families' incomes. Even when they work for low wages, Hispanics' buying power should not be discounted, because Hispanics have a tradition of "familia" and that means pooling resources. Individually, they may not appear qualified to buy high-ticket items, but collectively, they are.

In terms of marketing opportunities, one Hispanic group in particular warrants concentrated attention—the amnesty applicants. Some 2.7 million undocumented aliens from Mexico, South and Central America, and the Caribbean have submitted legalization applications under the nation's amnesty program. Once they feel safe with amnesty, many plan to buy homes, apply for credit cards, and purchase other big-ticket items. There is a window of opportunity if a company is alert and ready.

YOUTH

While nationally the general market is getting older, the Hispanic segment is a young population. The median age of the Hispanic market is 25.5 years compared with 32.2 years for the U. S. population as a whole. In fact, more than one-third (38.7 percent) of the Hispanic population is below the age of 20, according to the U. S. Bureau of the Census (August 1988B, 7). This fact has certainly not been missed by U. S. soft drink companies as well as toy and diaper manufacturers.

MARKET REALITIES

Many of the corporate executives I have worked with tend to judge the entire Hispanic segment by experience with one group. This is a form of stereotyping and a dangerous supposition. The Hispanic market has some twenty distinct and major submarkets within it, including 12.1 million people who trace their origins to Mexico, 2.5 million to Puerto Rico, one million to Cuba, and 2.2 million to Central and South American countries. Because of these subcultures within the Hispanic population, an East Coast-based company that has marketed for decades to New York's Puerto Rican community is not necessarily well equipped to devise an effective marketing strategy aimed at Southwest U. S. Hispanics of Mexican descent. National holidays, homeland affinities, traditions, foods, socioeconomic characteristics, geographic distribution, even language among these groups differ—sometimes dramatically. Many of the Cubans who fled from Castro's Cuba in the 1960s, for example, are middle-class. So if a company produces upscale products and services, it might want to specifically target these affluent and educated Cubans. However, if a company represents the grocery or toy business, it will want to target Mexicans who have much larger families than Cubans. If a company is pursuing the youth market, it is important to remember that there is a great variation in age among Hispanic ethnic groups. The oldest are Cubans with a median age of 38.7 years, and the youngest are Mexicans with a median age of 23.9 years and Puerto Ricans with a median age of 24.9 years.

Perhaps the greatest trap for companies seeking to attract Hispanic consumers is the difference in idioms and speaking styles between the subgroups. While nearly all Hispanics speak Spanish, half of all Hispanics reported that they had trouble understanding the Spanish of people whose country of origin differed from their own (Strategy Research Corp. 1984). It might be compared to an Englishman attempting to understand an American Southerner. A few businesses mounting national marketing campaigns have been sandbagged by the differences in idioms. In one case, a beverage company marketing a juice product found that Puerto Ricans understood the product had an orange flavor, while the Mexicans and Cubans understood it to have a "Chinese" flavor.

When planning a national Hispanic marketing campaign, a company needs to adopt "Walter Cronkite" Spanish—Spanish that everyone accepts and that avoids local idioms. Any script or written materials should be reviewed by Mexicans, Puerto Ricans, and Cubans to ensure that the wording is appropriate. Also, if food, music, or other cultural tie-ins are used in advertising, it should transcend identification with any one Spanish-origin group.

If, on the other hand, a company decides to appeal separately to each major Hispanic group, there are some cost-effective techniques that can be employed. A generic commerical aimed at Hispanics can be backed by different music tracks appealing to specific ethnic groups—perhaps Afro-Cuban music for Miami, salsa for New York's Puerto Ricans, and mariachi for Mexicans. On videos, ethnically distinct settings can be scissored in—a Cuban family can be depicted eating black beans and rice, while in another version, a Mexican family has tacos. Certainly, lifestyle approaches, such as sponsorship of a Paella

Festival in Flordia and the International Menudo Society community cookoffs in Los Angeles, are ways to reach distinct Hispanic subsegments. Paella, a rice dish with chicken and seafood, is a favorite of Cubans, while menudo is a traditional Mexican soup.

ASSIMILATION

A major marketing concern is assimilation. A 1986 Rand Corporation study of the effects of Mexican immigration on California concluded that Mexican immigrants are following the classic pattern for integrating into U. S. society, with education playing a critical role in this process (McCarthy and Valdez 1986). A somewhat different pattern was found in the *1989 U. S. Hispanic Market Study* conducted by Strategy Research Corporation. Researchers estimated that 13 percent of U. S. Hispanics have totally assimilated, meaning they have embraced the American culture on a day-to-day basis. Forty-nine percent were partially assimilated, meaning that they were generally fluent in English and might use it extensively in the work environment but tended to use Spanish at home. Thirty-eight percent were unassimilated, living totally immersed in Spanish language, media, products, civic organizations, and value systems.

In contrast to earlier European immigrants, Latinos benefit from continuing exposure to both Americas. Because of the proximity of Latin America and speed of travel, many Hispanics can travel easily back and forth between the United States and their native country. Mexicans frequently go across the border, while Puerto Ricans move easily between New York and San Juan. In addition, the large numbers and ongoing stream of newcomers from Latin America tend to keep earlier Hispanic immigrants aware of their heritage, language, and culture.

Other signs, however, point to increasing assimilation. The proportion of younger Hispanics who have completed high school is substantially higher than that of Hispanics aged 35 and older; more than one-half of all Hispanic women have joined their non-Hispanic counterparts in the work force; and there is frequent intermarriage between Hispanics and non-Hispanics.

Richard Lacayo observes that "one-third of all U. S. Hispanics intermarry with non-Hispanics, promising the day when the two cultures will be as tightly entwined as a strand of DNA" (1988, 47).

Part of this whole question of assimilation is the controversy over the use of English to reach Hispanic audiences. Atlhough most Hispanics prefer to speak Spanish at home, it is estimated that more than half are bilingual. In a study of California's Hispanics, researchers found the transition to English began almost immediately and proceeded very quickly. About half of the Hispanic immigrants living permanently in California and 90 percent of the first-generation U. S.-born Hispanics spoke English well. By the second generation, U. S.-born Hispanics were beginning to lose their bilingualism, with nearly half speaking only English (McCarthy and Valdez 1986). Herein is the dilemma. Hispanics do watch, listen to, and read Spanish-language media. Strategy Research Corporation found that two-thirds watch Spanish language television, about one-half listen to Spanish-language radio stations, and slightly more than one-fifth read Spanish language newspapers (Veciana-Suarez 1987, 4). But English-language media also accesses a substantial percentage of Hispanic households. In an *Adweek* article, editor Jack Feuer describes a BBDO Special Markets report which showed strong Hispanic viewership for such mainstream network shows as *The Cosby Show*. And then there is the traditional generation gap. "A kid 3 to 5 years old from a first generation family that has just crossed the border is never going to be found watching Spanish television. He's Americanized automatically," says comedian Paul Rodriguez. "His parents will watch the novelas" (Feuer 1989, 42–43).

There is also a growing number of glossy magazines, such as *Hispanic Business, Nuestro*, and the *Hispanic Review of Business* which are produced in English to appeal to the increasing number of upwardly mobile Hispanics who use English in conducting their business and professional lives.

Because of this fragmentation of Hispanic audiences, a media-driven approach, whether in English or Spanish, generally does not suffice. A bilingual approach is to be recommended.

LIFESTYLE APPROACHES

To effectively reach Hispanics, a company has to touch them in a number of ways—not only through English and Spanish media, but also through community events and educational programs integral to their lifestyles. One of our first Hispanic marketing programs introduced a major U.S. automobile company to the Hispanic population of Southern California through a series of community programs. In its "Vamos Juntos" (Going Places or On Our Way Up Together) campaign, the company co-sponsored Catholic church fiestas, picnics, and numerous other grass-roots events and launched a college scholarship program. In return for its help, local car dealers were permitted to bring their vehicles on-site during the events and have sales personnel on hand to answer questions. This program worked so well in raising the Hispanic community's awareness of the company that it was expanded to Texas, Chicago, and several other communities throughout the United States.

Values connections are essential in approaching the Hispanic community. The family and the Roman Catholic Church are very important to Hispanics. These commonalities, along with their strong work ethic, pride in their heritage, educational aspirations, enjoyment of public gatherings, enthusiasm for soccer, and love of music and the arts provide vehicles for reaching Hispanic consumers in a highly personal way.

CATHOLICISM

While many companies endlessly debate whether they should advertise in English or Spanish, they miss a lifestyle connection that is much stronger than language—the Catholic Church. Catholicism crosses all lines of Hispanic national origin and all levels of assimilation. Some 70 percent of all Hispanics are Roman Catholic. In the United States, one out of every four Catholics is Hispanic (Hansen 1988, 1), and if this trend continues, experts predict that by the year 2000, it will be one out of every three.

For most Hispanics, the local parish is far more than a Sunday of worship; it is the center of social groups, charitable activities, fiestas, and holiday celebrations. Even those Hispanics who do not practice Catholicism (the "Catholic cultured") are influenced by the church.

"LOS AMIGOS DE COMUNIDAD"

Working with Ralphs Grocery Company in California in the early 1980s, we helped create the "Los Amigos de Comunidad" (Friends of the Community) program, which links food retailers and such products as Tropicana Orange Juice, Coca-Cola, Ultra Pampers Plus, Maxwell House Coffee, and Mazola Oil with Hispanic communities.

Noting the success of the program in California, H. E. Butt Grocery Company, one of the largest independent retail grocery chains in Texas, decided to launch a "Los Amigos de Comunidad" program in South Texas. The company felt that direct grass-roots involvement is the most effective form of advertising, since it generates long-term loyalty among its customers. Now anchored by H. E. Butt Grocery Company in Texas and Ralphs Grocery Company in California, "Los Amigos" sponsor more than one hundred celebrations and fund-raising activities of Catholic churches and nonprofit organizations in high-density Hispanic communities in Texas and California. "Los Amigos" programs not only help with event promotion, but they provide donations of product and product gift certificates. For their assistance, sponsors receive recognition on banners and other promotional vehicles at the event and in retail grocery stores in Hispanic communities. They are also able to distribute samples to Hispanic consumers and access key influencers in Hispanic communities.

FAMILY TIES

The family has been accurately described as the "primal unit of Hispanic life" (Lacayo 1988, 49). Moreover, family to a Hispanic usually means grandparents, aunts, uncles, cousins, and even close friends. Not infrequently, three generations may live together in a household.

Attitudes toward members of the family may differ substantially from those of the general population. Although she may work outside the home, the Hispanic woman generally takes pride and pleasure in being a competent housewife and caregiver. Substantiating this difference was a survey in which many more Hispanics than non-Hispanics agreed with the statement that a woman's life is fulfilled only if she can provide a happy home for her family and that a married woman with children should not work outside the home unless extra money is needed (Strategy Research Corp. 1986, 433). Given these attitudes, portraying Hispanic women in advertising as harried, unfulfilled housewives will likely alienate them. A more appealing approach might be to show a mother teaching a child a family recipe and then serving the dish to the family. In its commercial spot for instant coffee, Hills Bros. Coffee showed Hispanic women as gracious hostesses and garnered a 20 percent increase in sales (Cuneo 1989, S-1).

The elderly in Hispanic families, as in Asian-American families, are generally honored rather than regarded as burdens. Grandparents, great aunts, and other elderly family members are perceived as wise people who are integrally involved in family life. Children in the Hispanic family are generally disciplined when necessary and expected to carry their own load, but they are also cherished and treated with affection.

To build upon the strong family orientation of Hispanics, Sears, Roebuck & Company and Eastman Kodak Company, among others, participate with the Hispanic American Family of the Year Foundation in sponsoring family fairs and Hispanic American Family of the Year recognition dinners.

"The Foundation seeks to enhance the image of Hispanic-American families by demonstrating how they contribute to making the United States a better nation and to upgrade the quality of life for all Hispanic-American families," explains Bernie Kemp, chairman of the board for the foundation. "Our family fairs include emphasis on employment opportunities in the public and private sectors, health screenings and vaccinations, and workshops on such topics as encouraging young people to stay in school and out of gangs" (Kemp 1989).

Recognition dinners held in California, Texas, Illinois, and Florida, honor Hispanic-American families nominated by community groups or others for their community service, team work, cultural pride, and family values.

Company sponsors for these programs help with promotional and administrative costs, donate prizes such as a shopping spree at Sears for the "family of the year," and provide college scholarships. Benefits to the companies include exposure in *Hispanic American Family* magazine and in press coverage of the events, in-store events honoring the "families of the year," improved visibility in Hispanic markets, and a strengthening of ties with Hispanics throughout the United States (Kemp 1989).

Well aware that Hispanics are family-oriented, Frito-Lay developed its "Parque de la Amistad" (Park of Friendship) promotion. The company supported the building of playgrounds and parks in Hispanic neighborhoods by donating twenty cents for every empty bag of Frito-Lay products redeemed at participating stores. In Houston, Texas, the promotion raised $15,000, and local community groups and businesses donated another $15,000. Some five hundred volunteers, including Frito-Lay representatives, showed up to help work on the park. Not only did the program create good will for Frito-Lay, it also boosted sales. Researchers found that Frito-Lay's brand awareness increased by up to 12 percent among Hispanic consumers and purchases increased by up to 14 percent (Schwartz 1989, 45).

Beyond community events, several companies employ family themes in their advertising to Hispanics. Eastman Kodak shows a mother and father taking pictures of their child at a school open house. Polaroid shows a family in the hospital with a newborn child and Polaroid photos spread out on the bed (Weinstein 1989, S-2). A Toyota television spot shows a pregnant woman being taken to the hospital accompanied by her mother-in-law (Stroud 1989, S-9). In one of its commercials, McDonald's depicts a family celebrating a 15-year-old girl's birthday. A *quinceañera* celebrates the traditional coming of age for Hispanic women. Generally, companies that build upon the

closeness of the family are likely to be well received by the
Hispanic consumer.

EDUCATION

Like many immigrant groups before them, Hispanic families
value education. In fact, many immigrants came to the United
States for the express purpose of getting an education. Strategy
Research Corporation found that Hispanics much more than
their non-Hispanic counterparts believe a college degree is important in today's society.

Hispanics are, according to the U.S. Bureau of the Census
(August 1989(B), 4), becoming increasingly better educated. In
1988, the proportion of younger Hispanics who had completed
at least four years of high school was 62 percent compared with
44 percent among Hispanics 35 years of age and older. And the
proportion of college graduates was 12 percent compared with
9 percent among older Hispanics. Certainly, these figures por-
tend increased buying power as Hispanics ascend the socioeconomic ladder.

Beverage companies have been quick to tap into the educational aspirations of Hispanics. Pepsi-Cola has been particularly active in this area. It produced public service announce-
ments featuring Hispanic celebrities urging young Hispanics to
stay in school. Other companies have also capitalized on educational concerns. Financial planners, for example, have written articles in Hispanic magazines, explaining how funds can
be accumulated for the children's college educations by invest-
ing in mutual funds and zero-coupon bonds.

SOCCER

Raised playing soccer in Mexico and South America, many
Latinos continue to nurture their interest in the sport after they
arrive in the United States. There are local soccer leagues for
age groups ranging from youth to adult, and often the teams
and leagues are organized along the lines of national origin.

Convinced early on of the wisdom of reaching Hispanics through soccer, Ford Motor Company became involved as a major sponsor of amateur soccer in the United States and enlisted Pelé as its celebrity spokesperson. In the early 1980s, we linked Ford Motor Company and Partners Assisting Recreation Through Cooperative Support (PARCS), a nonprofit organization affiliated with Los Angeles County Parks and Recreation. This linkage further cemented the connection between Ford and soccer. Each year, Ford donates money toward the maintenance and upgrading of the Ford/Pelé Soccer Center in South El Monte, California. In a related program, Ford combines education and soccer through its sponsorship of the Ford/Pelé college scholarships.

"Since the inception of the program in 1984, Ford has donated $1,000 college scholarships to 45 young people who have been involved in bonafide soccer programs. Most of the young people are Hispanics," explains Ilona Volkman, scholarship coordinator.

Ford's involvement is more than financial. Company executives serve as part of the judging committee and participate in the recognition and awards ceremony luncheon for the scholarship winners and their families. Pelé often participates in these luncheons and spends hours signing autographs. For its efforts, Ford receives recognition in the Hispanic community, since the scholarship winners are formally presented with plaques at their high school or college student body assemblies and at a meeting of the Los Angeles County Board of Supervisors. The attendant press coverage for these events also enhances Ford's image among Hispanics (Volkman 1989).

Along with Ford, Procter & Gamble Company is also capitalizing on the soccer connection. The company sponsored the Clasico International soccer tour which attracted one hundred thousand people (Edel 1989, S-14).

CULTURAL PRIDE

A cornerstone of Hispanic communities throughout the United States is their pride in their culture and desire to keep it alive in their adopted country. "Hispanics want to belong to America without betraying the past. Yet we fear losing ground in any negotiation with America. Our fear, most of all, is of losing our culture," warns writer Richard Rodriguez (1988, 84). Other Hispanics echo these thoughts. More than nine out of ten Hispanics questioned by researchers said they were proud to be Hispanic and thought their culture, language, and traditions should be preserved. This high level of cultural pride is characteristic of all Hispanics, regardless of their national origin.

Richard Lacayo notes that even with the diversity of Hispanic cultures, there is a common thread in the reverence for the past. "The U.S. is a nation that puts no great premium on the past. . . . But Hispanic culture is consumed with the past on both the personal and historical levels and drawn to the memory play, the history painting, the musical tradition to accomplish the tasks of recollection" (1988, 48).

To recall the richness of their past and retain their traditions, Hispanic communities throughout the country turn out for parades and celebrations honoring their heritage. Sponsorship involvement in these celebrations is an ideal way for a company to establish a presence in a local Hispanic community. Among the most popular events are Carnaval Miami in Florida; the Puerto Rican Day and Hispanic Day Parades in New York; the Hispanic American Festival in Washington, D.C.; Fiesta del Sol in Chicago; and Charro Days in Brownsville, Texas. Pepsi-Cola has found these events to be ideal vehicles for targeting the different subsegments of the Hispanic market, sponsoring El Diez y Seis de Setiembre celebrations to appeal to Mexicans and Calle Ocho to appeal to Cubans. September 16 is a Mexican holiday commemorating the time when Father Miguel de Hidalgo declared Mexico's independence in 1810, while Calle Ocho is a major celebration in Miami.

When a company participates in these events, it must do more than just hang banners or put its name on a float. The effectiveness of the exposure is magnified when it is combined with a benefit for the Hispanic community. For instance, CPC International's Mazola cooking oil not only sponsors several Carnaval Miami events each year, it also returns proceeds from some contests to Hispanic charities (Freeman 1988, S-12). Another way to stand out at these celebrations is to become the sole or primary sponsor of an event, and do so year after year.

At the heart of Hispanic cultural identity is love of the visual arts, the dramatic arts, Latin music, and dancing.

"The arts are exceedingly important to Hispanics," explains Carman Zapata, an actress and producing director of the Bilingual Foundation of the Arts. "The arts bring Hispanics together and enable them to celebrate their heritage and culture and build their self-esteem. A people with out a culture are a people who are dead inside" (Zapata 1989).

From the murals on buildings and storm drains in Los Angeles to the Museum of Contemporary Hispanic Art in New York City, the emotional affinity of Hispanics for the visual arts and vibrant colors is obvious. McDonald's employed the art connection by sponsoring an Hispanic Heritage Art Contest in the mid-1980s. The contest conducted with the cooperation of the schools in Hispanic communities garnered extensive exposure for McDonald's—not only in Hispanic neighborhoods but also nationally. The prize-winning entries were displayed in the Capitol Children's Museum in Washington, D.C., and grandprize winners presented their drawings to President Reagan during Hispanic Heritage Week. More recently, Adolph Coors Company sponsored an exhibit of Hispanic art, Expresiónes Hispana, which has toured the country.

Whether it is mariachi with its guitar-accompanied Mexican folk songs or salsa with its blending of African music, rock n' roll, and big band brass, Hispanics respond to music and seek to preserve their musical heritage. Four out of five Hispanics, coming from different countries, said they like listening to Latin music and more than three out of four enjoy dancing to Latin rhythms, according to Strategy Research Corporation's *1987 U.S. Hispanic Market Study* (1986, 425). Beverage companies have been at the forefront of using music to appeal to the Hispanic segment. Pepsi-Cola has relied on the "Latin American Music Awards," "Domingos Alegres," "Muy Especial," "Video Éxitos," and other musical programs to attract young Hispanics who may not watch much Spanish-language television. It also appealed to the bilingual segment of the U.S. Hispanic population by creating English language versions of its commercial

featuring Gloria Estefan and the Miami Sound Machine, a popular Hispanic music group. The commercial served double duty,
since the Miami Sound Machine has tremendous appeal to non-
Hispanics as well (Elizalde 1987, 8, 9). Coca-Cola USA has also
been involved with the "Tejano Music Awards," and Budweiser Beer sponsored the International Salsa Festival. Other
industries are gradually following the beverage companies' lead.
In Los Angeles, for example, GTE sponsored OTI, an international Spanish songwriting competition.

An unusual program that reaches both Hispanics and non-
Hispanics is the Bilingual Foundation of the Arts in Los Angeles. The 16-year-old nonprofit organization provides three plays
a season, ranging from dramas written during Spain's Golden
Age to those authored by emerging Hispanic-American play-
wrights. It also sponsors a Reader's Theater for new works.
These plays are performed alternately in English and Spanish
(Zapata 1989). A new project of the foundation is a children's
theater, "Teatro Para Los Niños". In the children's theater,
original plays with a substantial musical element are performed. "The adult performers speak both English and Spanish in the same play," says Pablo Marz, director (1989). "More
than 50,000 children in the Los Angeles city and county schools
have seen the plays, and children in Chicago and Texas will
now have the same opportunity."

Corporations including R. J. Reynolds Tobacco Company,
Atlantic Richfield Company, Xerox Corporation, and J. C. Pen-
ney Company, Inc. have long sponsored the foundation through
grants. Additionally, some corporate executives serve on its
board of directors or as volunteers for special projects.

Rewards for the sponsors include mention in playbills, banners, publicity releases, acknowledgment at fund-raising dinners, and the like. Zapata (1989) believes that a more subtle
benefit is that the sponsoring corporations are getting name
and product exposure at a time when Hispanic consumers are
receptive. "These corporations are reaching people at times when
they feel good inside and when they are proud of their heritage," she says.

THE HISPANIC WORK ETHIC

When Hispanic immigrants are asked why they are coming to the United States, one of the most prevalent answers is, "I came to work." Generally, Hispanics believe there are more economic opportunities in the United States and that they can advance through hard work. And whatever their occupation, be it laborer, manager, or professional, most do work hard. But they also do not usually become "workaholics," placing equal value on family time.

Nearly 360,000 Hispanics have plugged into America's capitalist system by starting their own businesses and generating some $20 billion in annual revenues (Barber 1988). While many of these businesses are such "mom and pop" enterprises as landscaping/gardening, auto repair, bakeries, light construction, and small restaurants, others are banks, medical centers, and legal services centers.

Reaching Hispanics through their work ethic is another opportunity for a company to gain market share in this segment. The U.S. Hispanic Chamber of Commerce is an attractive route used by such major corporations as Eastman Kodak Company, McDonald's Corporation, Chrysler Corporation, and American Telephone & Telegraph Company. They have all had booths at the chamber's national convention as a means of wooing Hispanic employees, subcontractors, and customers, as well as demonstrating their support for the Hispanic segment's economic aspirations.

It is obvious that companies cannot assume that general market ads or approaches will automatically reach the Hispanic segment. Hispanic culture, values, and attitudes are strong. Fortunately, there are great commonalities among all U.S. Hispanics—the family, the Catholic Church, the work and educational aspirations, and the respect for their heritage. By building lifestyle programs around these commonalities, a company can deliver the message that it cares and wants to be accepted as an *amigo* (friend) in Hispanic comunities.

AFRICAN AMERICANS

While the mass media probes the plight of the urban African-American poor, it rarely reports the movement of millions of African Americans into the nation's financial mainstream. Many African Americans are managers of department stores and corporate branch offices, owners of businesses, teachers, doctors, nurses, real estate brokers, and financial planners. In addition to this rising middle class, a number of African Americans have entered the ranks of the wealthy. There are now hundreds of African Americans among the estimated one million families worth more than $1 million in the United States (*EBONY*, October 1988, 166).

These points are important because too often corporate America neglects African-American consumers, turning its attention instead to the pursuit of the faster-growing Hispanic or higher-income Asian segments.

To overlook the nation's largest minority, numbering 30.7 million, is a strategic mistake. Consider that:

- The African-American consumer market is projected to rise from an estimated $240 billion to $660 billion by the year 2000, according to several economic studies.
- Roughly one-third of all African-American households

have incomes of $25,000 or more, and one out of thir-
teen (7.5 percent) have incomes of $50,000 or more (U.S.
Bureau of Census, February 1989, 13).

- African-American consumers spend an estimated $34.5
billion on food products, $12.8 billion on clothing and
accessories, $14.3 billion on automobiles and trucks, $3.3
billion on personal care and services, $6.2 billion on
home furnishings and equipment, $3.5 billion on dif-
ferent forms of insurance, $2.6 billion on non-alcoholic
beverages, and $2.4 billion on alcoholic products
(*EBONY*, May 1989, 23).

- Since 1970, the African-American population has grown
at about twice the rate of the white population. Between now and the year 2030, the U.S. Bureau of the
Census projects that the African-American (black) population will increase by nearly half—some 14 million
people (January 1989, 90).

This statistical summary reveals the strength of the African-
American consumer market. And this market becomes increasingly more important during these times of single-digit sales
growth and increased competition.

MARKET PARTICULARITIES

Not only the size and spending clout of the African-American consumer segment but also its distinctive characteristics—
its relative youth, the impact of female decision makers, and
geographical clustering—are important considerations a company must keep in mind.

The African-American population is considerably younger than
the white population. Nearly half (46 percent) of the African-
American population is under the age of 25. Even the median
age of African-Americans (27.2 years) is five years less than the
median age of the white population (U.S. Bureau of the Census, March 1988, 5, 11). Because of the age differences, more
African-American consumers are expected to continue the freer-
spending lifestyles of younger age groups.

In the African-American market, women have considerable clout. A sizable share of the market is comprised of female-headed households. The percentage of African-American families maintained by women has increased sharply in recent decades; 43 percent of all African-American families are headed by women with no husband present (U.S. Bureau of the Census, February 1989, 3). The market is also skewed to the feminine side, with African-American females outnumbering African-American males 16.1 million to 14.6 million. Some marketing experts recommend that African-American women be considered a subsegment of the total African-American population. "Single or married, with or without children, she is a significant decision maker in her household," explains expert Sheila Gadsden (1985, 18). What is missing, according to Gadsden, is visible marketing efforts that reach her both as a woman who is black and a woman who is spending money.

The geographic pattern of African Americans is significant in the U.S. market. A reverse migration of African Americans is occurring. In the 1940s, there was a large movement of African Americans from the South to the industrial area of the North. But since 1973, a number of African Americans have been returning to the South. In 1987, 56 percent of all African Americans lived in the South, up from 52 percent in 1980. And by the year 2000, the U.S. Bureau of the Census estimates that African Americans will make up at least one-fourth or more of the population in Mississippi (36 percent), Louisiana (32 percent), South Carolina (30 percent), Maryland (28 percent), Georgia (27 percent), and Alabama (26 percent)(Schwartz 1989, 13). Also by the turn of the century, more than one-third of the nation's African-American population will live in New York (3.2 million), California (2.9 million), Texas (2.4 million), Florida (2.3 million), and Georgia (2.2 million). African Americans will be the major racial group in such key U.S. cities as Detroit, Baltimore, Memphis, Washington, D.C., New Orleans, Newark, and Atlanta.

WHAT'S THE RIGHT APPROACH?

Decades after the Civil Rights Act was passed in 1964, companies are still grappling with how to approach the African-American consumer market.

One of the most obvious considerations is the sensitivity of African Americans to any signs of racism and stereotyping. Little Black Sambo and black servant mammies have long since disappeared from print ads and commercials, but more subtle forms of prejudice still exist. The portrayal of African Americans in subordinate roles or the injection of "right on, brother" or "honey chil' " into ads are guaranteed to offend most African-American consumers.

In consumer focus groups, African Americans say they want to see themselves portrayed as healthy people in upscale settings to which they can relate or aspire—in other words, living out the American Dream. Depicting a middle-aged woman in graduation robes with diploma in hand, a couple admiring their new washing machine, and parents tenderly holding their infant son are some of the positive ways companies have appealed to this consumer segment.

Black or African American?

"Colored," "Negro," "Afro-American," and "black" have all been descriptive terms used in marketing and advertising. There is currently a movement to replace the term "black" with "African American." The Rev. Jesse Jackson and several prominent African Americans have announced a preference for the term "African American," pointing out that every ethnic group in the United States has a reference to some cultural base. Others argue that given the presence of blacks from the West Indies and other regions, the term "African American" is inappropriate. Despite their objections, usage of the term "African American" seems to be increasing.

Targeted or General Media

While the general mass media does reach African-American consumers, the African-American media can help ensure that a company's message gets across. Several African-American-oriented publications have major national circulations. *EBONY*, for instance, reaches some 40 percent of African-American adults. The African-American electronic media is estimated to reach 70 percent of African-American U.S. households (Pfaff and Fannin 1986, 44). Sharing the mission of progress for the African-American movement, the African-American media is often a strong ally in creating special programs to appeal to African-American consumers. The financial services company of Dean Witter Reynolds, Inc., for example, teamed up with *Black Enterprise*, a magazine for African-American businessmen and professionals, to sponsor a series of one-day seminars on personal, financial, and career planning in major cities across the country.

CELEBRITY MARKETING

One technique that works well in both African-American and general media and special events programming is the use of African-American celebrities. The marketing advantages of using celebrities are many, including rapid establishment of credibility and name recognition within the African-American community and a preemptive position that would be difficult if not impossible for competitors to duplicate. The affiliation of rock star Michael Jackson and Pepsi-Cola, for example, preempts arch competitor Coca-Cola from doing the same.

An effective use of celebrity endorsements is to find those superstars who appeal to both African Americans and the general public. Entertainers like Bill Cosby and sports heroes like Isiah Thomas have cross-over followings.

But while celebrity endorsements are effective, they are not cure-alls for cultivating the African-American consumer. These endorsements need to be linked with grass-roots programs that benefit the African-American community and are consistent with lifestyles. We used this combined technique in a marketing program linking Walter Payton, one of the greatest running backs in the history of football, with Energizer Batteries and Wilson Sporting Goods. To enhance Energizer's exposure and image in the Chicago area, which has large minority populations, we organized an Energizer Battery/Walter Payton Youth Sports program. In exchange for empty Energizer battery packs, the program supplied badly needed sports equipment to the Chicago inner-city schools and youth groups. Grass-roots awareness was stimulated through program materials and posters distributed in Chicago's inner-city schools and clubs and T-shirts emblazoned with "Walter Payton & ENERGIZER Youth Sports program."

LIFESTYLE APPROACHES

In discussing the survival of black America, historian Lerone Bennett, Jr., reveals a significant lifestyle connections to the African-American community: "If blacks are alive and reasonably well today . . . it is because of the extended black family and house rent parties and church suppers and black schools and black churches" (1986, 128).

AFRICAN-AMERICAN CHURCHES

Churches occupy positions of prominence in the African-American community, perhaps because they are among the few institutions that African Americans have been free to control.

"Black churches have been safe havens from the pain and strife of life in the outside world, sponsors of educational institutions, social welfare agencies, missionary headquarters for proselytizing in Africa, depositories of corporate wealth, and initiators of lucrative business enterprises," notes historian Harold Cruse in *Plural but Equal* (1987, 230).

Churches also have long been at the forefront in the struggle for equal rights and improved conditions. Beginning in the last 1950s, the Southern Christian Leadership Conference (SCLC), formed by the Revs. E. D. Nixon, Ralph Abernathy, and Martin Luther King, Jr., led thousands of African Americans in demonstrations against segregation laws.

Examples abound of the African-American churches' integral role in all aspects of community life. In Washington, D.C., Shiloh Baptist Church has been combatting social ills since the congregation was organized by former slaves in 1863. The church now sponsors some ninety groups focusing on the problems and concerns of the African-American family, ranging from tutorial programs to job counseling (*EBONY* 1986, 158). The Congress of National Black Churches (CNBC), an umbrella organization for some 65,000 churches, spearheaded the founding of Project Spirit, a pilot program of after-school tutorials aimed at improving the academic skills of elementary school students and making them more aware of their cultural heritage. CNBC also launched a national anti-drug abuse campaign. In Chicago, Project IMAGE, a consortium of ten churches, seeks to strengthen the role of African-American males by addressing the need for positive male influences among African-American boys. In New York, Concord Baptist Church has a $1-million "Christfund" to help finance the local Billie Holiday Theater for young performing artists, among other projects (Poinsett 1988, 144). In Durham, North Carolina, the African-American churches are a vehicle for promoting health and fitness with a Fitness Through Churches project that trains congregation members to be exercise instructors and health advocates (Olson 1989, 194). Support for any one of these programs would bring the sponsor not only high visibility and community appreciation, but also contacts with the "influentials" of the African-American segment.

THE EXTENDED FAMILY

The backbone of the African-American community is the extended family, and it has a long history. Slave children were taught to respect and revere older persons whom they called "aunt" and "uncle"; it was customary for adult slaves to call each other "brother" and "sister" and to look upon each other's children mutually as their own (Bennett 1986, 124). Most African Americans today still rely on family and relatives for the care of their children rather than formal day-care programs. A report by Impact Resources found that middle-class African Americans often continue to live with relatives, and because they do so, they may actually have more discretionary income than white consumers of comparable income levels (Shiver 1989, IV-8).

Recognizing the importance of the extended family to African-American consumers, General Foods Corporation sponsored a "Family Reunion Sweepstakes," providing winners with $25,000 worth of travel and hotel accommodations for their next family reunion. McDonald's built upon the extended family theme in its commercial which showed a young man taking his grandmother out to eat.

An amplification of the extended family emphasis is found in the mutual aid and sociopolitical action organizations of the African-American community. These include the National Urban League, the National Association for the Advancement of Colored People (NAACP), Operation PUSH (People United to Save Humanity), the National Council of Negro Women, the Links, Inc., Jack & Jill of America, and the Greek letter organizations, including Alpha Kappa Alpha, Delta Sigma Theta, Zeta Phi Beta, and Sigma Gamma Rho sororities and the Alpha Phi Alpha, Phi Beta Sigma, Kappa Alpha Psi, and Omega Psi Phi fraternities. These groups have all developed programs to benefit African-American families and the community as a whole. For instance, Omega Psi Phi has organized health fairs, employment seminars, Project Manhood for males aged 10 to 16, and a Summer Leadership Development Conference for college-bound juniors and seniors (*EBONY*, August 1988, 162).

These organizations present opportunities for extensive, long-term alliances with the African-American segment. Beverage and food companies have signed agreements with Operation PUSH to fund educational programs, sporting teams, and cultural events. And some forty companies nationwide have signed "Fair Share Agreements" with the NAACP, promising to expand opportunities for African Americans in employment, purchasing, and other economic areas (Westerman 1989, 32).

EDUCATION

In its annual reader's poll, *EBONY* asked readers what issue should be the president's greatest priority concern for African Americans. Education was near the top of the list, second only to unemployment (*EBONY*, May 1989, 202).

Although educational opportunities for African Americans are improving in some areas, they are stagnating in others. The number of young African Americans graduating from high school has been increasing, climbing from 53 percent in 1970 to 82 percent in 1987 (Bennett 1988, 4). But while the number of African-American youths eligible for college has risen, the number who actually go on has barely held steady.

By helping to ease the financial constraints that often keep talented African-American high school graduates from entering college, a company can be perceived as a caring partner. Beverage companies, including soft-drink companies that target the young consumer, have been particularly active in the education arena, sponsoring scholarships and stay-in-school programs. Coca-Cola USA developed its Share a Dream Scholarship program to commemorate the national observance of Martin Luther King, Jr.'s birthday. Since its inception in 1982, the program has awarded $750,000 in scholarships. In its 1989 promotion, Coca-Cola increased the appeal of its program by featuring three prominent African-American athletes who symbolize the value of education—Julius "Dr. J" Erving, Michael Jordan, and Isiah Thomas (*Jet* 1989, 32). PepsiCo sponsored a Lionel Ritchie "Stay in School" tour (Westerman 1989, 32). Miller Brewing Company became a founding sponsor of the Thurgood Marshall Black Education Fund which helps send young African Americans to predominantly African-American public colleges.

Recognizing that the majority of African-American college graduates have come from the 115 historically and prominently African-American colleges, corporations such as Anheuser-

Busch, Inc., the Kellogg Company, American Airlines Inc., Polaroid Corporation, Amoco Corporation, Eastman Kodak Company, and American Telephone & Telegraph Company have
supported the United Negro College Fund. Some corporations
have not only donated money, but have also developed summer internship programs for the students and set up mentor
programs.

One of the more creative marketing approaches is that of In-
diana National Bank, which launched an America's Black Colleges Affinity Card program. The bank issues a Visa card in-
scribed with the name of a participating institution. Alumni and
supporters of participating colleges and universities who have
approved credit receive a free Visa card for the first year. The
educational institution receives a fee for each approved account, and each time the card is used for a purchase, the bank
pays a percentage of each transaction to the college or the National Association for Equal Opportunity in Higher Education
(NAFEO).

HISTORY, TRADITIONS, AND ACHIEVEMENTS

Much of what appeals to African Americans is based on a
respect for their heritage. "Knowing our roots gives us the appreciation and self-esteem necessary to build upon this valuable legacy," the Rev. Jesse Jackson says (1989, 190).

How can a company develop tie-ins with African-American
history, culture, and achievements? Black History Month celebrated every February and Martin Luther King, Jr. Day celebrated in January provide focal points. Kodak's Professional
Photography Division and U.S. West supported a photography
exhibition featuring seventy-five portraits of African-American
women, including the first African-American women president
of a college and entertainer Leontyne Price. The exhibition, "I
Dream a World: Portraits of Black Women Who Changed
America," opened in Washington, D.C., during Black History
Month, and then began a two-year tour through twenty states
(Barras 1989, 33). Incidentally, this exhibit not only garnered
Kodak publicity in the African-American media but in a major

article of *U.S. News & World Report* as well. Philip Morris Company, Inc., helped the Congress of Racial Equality (CORE) stage a Martin Luther King birthday celebration in New York (Miller 1989, 20). Miller Brewing Company sponsored an exhibition honoring African-American attorneys who have made significant contributions to the Civil Rights movement (Barras 1989, 34).

Interestingly, states as well as businesses are capitalizing on African-American culture and history as a way to reach African Americans. To increase tourism, the state of Ohio published a Heritage Trails brochure, featuring African-American historical attractions, and runs ads promoting the brochure in *American Visions*, a magazine of African-American culture. Similarly, the Greater New Orleans Tourist & Convention Commission issued a brochure on the black heritage of New Orleans.

THE ARTS

Whatever its form—jazz, blues, gospel, rap, pop—music is an integral part of the African-American experience. And such African-American entertainers as Stevie Wonder, Lionel Hampton, Etta James, B. B. King, the Pointer Sisters, and Whitney Houston have enhanced not only the lives of African Americans but of all Americans.

Aware that music is a vital link to the African-American consumer, Kentucky Fried Chicken sponsors an annual Gospel Music Festival which involves hundreds of gospel choirs. Sony Corporation of America has an annual competition that salutes new talent in the fields of music and film (Barras 1989, 31). In general television advertising, major corporations have used music to create an underlying appeal to African-American consumers. Levi Strauss employed a jazzy musical background for its 501 jeans commercial, and Wendy's International Inc., had an African-American saxophonist play a blues version of its theme for the television spot promoting its breakfast service.

Beyond music, there are countless other forms of artistic expression which a company might support: dance, theater, creative writing, photography, painting, or sculpture. The

American Telephone & Telegraph Foundation helps a variety of African-American organizations, including the New Jersey's Crossroad's Theatre, the Dallas Black Dance Theater, the Dance Theatre of Harlem, and the Alvin Ailey Dance Company. McDonald's has its Literary Achievement Awards presented in cooperation with the Negro Ensemble Company of New York. National winners in poetry, fiction, and playwriting get a trip to New York and have celebrities, such as Phylicia Rashad, co-star of "The Cosby Show," read their works (Barras 1989, 34).

If a company is local rather than national, it can still partici-pate in sponsorships. First Interstate Bank of California and the California State Lottery were among the sponsors of "Intro-spectives: Contemporary Art by Americans and Brazilians of African Descent" at the California Afro-American Museum in Los Angeles.

SPORTS

Sports is a powerful lifestyle affinity tool to reach targeted market segments, and this is particularly true for reaching the African-American consumer. The achievements of African-American athletes in the Olympics, basketball, baseball, foot-ball, track and field, and numerous other sports are a source of continuing pride and self-esteem for African Americans. Seeing sports as a vehicle for social and economic mobility, African-American families often encourage their children to pursue sports careers. Sports programs for youth help build trust relation-ships with the African-American community. Hershey Foods Corporation has a National Track and Field Youth program which has as its spokesperson Rafer Johnson, 1960 Olympic gold medalist. McDonald's sponsors an all-American high school basketball team, most of whose members are African American. Coca-Cola and Henessey in 1988 gave the Visions Foundation money to bring together the country's past Afri-can-American Olympic winners (Barras 1989, 35). African-American athletes appear in numerous ads designed to appeal to the African-American consumer. World champion Jackie Joyner Kersee is shown relying on Primatene Mist when she has an asthma attack, "Dr. J" prescribes Dr. Scholl's for athlete's foot, and Isiah Thomas, an eight-time NBA All Star, talks about the All-Star quality of the Toyota Camry.

To reach African-American consumers requires a willingness to do more than place a black model in a white ad or buy a ticket to an NAACP dinner. It requires a willingness to develop ads, programs, and special events that relate to African-Americans' history, heroes, cherished institutions, culture, and emotional needs.

MARKETING THROUGH SPORTS

Sports and recreational activities are potent lifestyle affinity tools for reaching nearly every segment of the American marketplace. Polo and yachting attract the very rich while golf attracts the professionals, affluent, and secure adults. Older women enjoy synchronized swimming and fitness walking. Yuppies ski and run marathons, while their children play more soccer than baseball in some regions.

In a *Business Week* cover story, Michael Oneal and co-authors maintained that "nothing sells like sports" (1987, 48). And it is not only professional sports that sell. Organized amateur sports, youth participation sports, young adult intramural sports, and recreational and fitness activities can all be in a company's sports marketing armamentarium. The reason for this broad sports emphasis is that the U.S. population is becoming a participatory society. No longer interested in just being spectators at sporting events, Americans in increasing numbers are participants.

One measure of Americans' passion for sports is how much they spend on everything from ski lift tickets to baseball cards. The dollar figures are astronomical. *Sports inc* estimates that Americans spend $47.25 billion a year on sports, more than one percent of the Gross National Product (*Time* 1987, 52). The growth in the number of sports and fitness-related magazines is another key indicator. *Baseball Digest, Bicycling, Body Boarding, Bowling, Canoe, City Sports, Executive Golfer, Golf, Rider, Runner's World, Ski, Sports Illustrated, Surfer Magazine, Tavern Sports, Tennis, Triathlete Magazine*—the list goes on and on.

For some industries, a particular sport has become a virtual "meal ticket" to key consumer segments. More than three-quarters of the golf courses built in the United States are associated with the real estate development industry. "The developers are building the courses not because they are convinced that golf is a good business to be in, but because they realize that a course significantly enhances the value of a piece of land" (*Sports inc* 1988, 20).

TRENDS

The Fitness Emphasis

The increased awareness of fitness in America, involving both men and women, has spawned the era of the "grass-roots sports" enthusiast. Among Americans 25 and older, one out of every five participates in a major fitness activity at least two times a week, according to the National Sporting Goods Association Survey (Doyle 1989, 38). This figure is consistent throughout all groups. When occasional participants are considered, the percentages climb even higher.

Of key interest to marketers is that the types of activities selected by frequent participants vary according to gender, age, and income. Men more often prefer to jog and exercise with equipment, while women are more likely to be involved in aerobics, exercise walking, and cycling. Nearly one-half the exercise walkers are aged 55 and older, while more than one-half (53.4 percent) of the joggers are aged 25 to 34. About one-third (30.4 percent) of all joggers have incomes of $50,000 or more. Obviously, the demographic profiles of the participants in each activity enables companies to target specific customers much more effectively. But before a company focuses on one sport, it needs to recognize that target customers could be involved in more than one activity. In other words, marketing to the lifestyle of skiers may very well mean addressing the probability that they are also pursuing interests in cycling, running, and swimming.

Women in Sports

The number of women who participate in sports has exploded since 1972 when Title IX of the Educational Amendments Act went into effect. That amendment requires that schools receiving federal aid offer to women sports scholarships, teams, coaches, uniforms, and athletic facilities equal to those of men. As programs for girls and women have grown throughout the country, the number of women athletes and sports fans continues to grow. Some 1.8 million girls participated in thirty-two high school sports during the 1988-89 school year, according to the National Federation of State High School Association's sports participation survey. Basketball was the most popular girls' high school sport, followed by track and field, volleyball, fast-pitch softball, and tennis (Upton 1989). On college campuses across the country, more than eighty thousand female students play on varsity teams in sports ranging from volleyball to ice hockey (Lichtenstein 1989, 202). Female athletes are becoming sports celebrities and local and national television stations have begun airing women's collegiate basketball, volleyball, gymnastics, and softball games.

Beyond college sports, women are taking up recreational sports in increasing numbers. More than 40 percent of new golfers are women (*Sports inc* 1988, 20), and women bowlers now outnumber male bowlers, 26 million to 22 million (Goulian 1988, 48).

As the importance of sports in reaching women of all ages becomes recognized, more and more companies have signed on as sponsors. The pioneers—Virginia Slims and Reebok International—have been joined by several others. Eastman Kodak Company, for example, focused on women's basketball in its sponsorship of the 1990 Goodwill Games in Seattle, Washington, while Wendy's chose women's volleyball (McManus 1989, 20).

Take Your Pick

Restrictions on commercialism in sports are being overturned today. Over the last decade, the limits on commercialism in the Olympics have eased so much that by 1988, nine companies paid the International Olympic Committee $120 million for worldwide rights to link their corporate logos to the games. Countless others signed less expensive agreements with the U.S. and other Olympic committees, sports federations, teams, and individual athletes.

The military, too, has done an about face. When new regulations regarding sponsorship of recreational activities on military bases became effective in 1988, several major corporations were on hand to capitalize on the opportunity. Domino's Pizza sponsored the Army's men's and women's softball games at Fort Bliss in El Paso, Texas. Previously, the military had been barred from actively recruiting corporate sponsors for its $1.6-billion morale, welfare, and recreation program (Meyers 1989). The armed services could accept funding from unsolicited sponsors, but the sponsors were prohibited from advertising the upcoming events on television or other media in the local market. Current regulations allow corporate sponsors to promote their sponsorships through advertising and product sampling, rather than being silent contributors.

The U.S. Military Academy and U.S. Naval Academy are permitting corporate sponsorships of their annual football games. Sponsors get exclusive use of the Army and Navy logos in point of purchase sales, rights to conduct pregame hospitality events, and a specified number of tickets (Dunavant 1989, 56).

Until recent years, corporate sponsorship of a major league baseball team might mean sponsoring a bat day. As baseball commissioner, Peter Uberroth established a corporate marketing program that put millions of dollars in the pockets of the clubs. In 1989 alone baseball received some $14 billion from eight national sponsors and several million dollars more through local sponsorship programs. The Equitable Financial Companies, IBM, General Motors Corporation (Chevrolet), Leaf Inc., MasterCard International, Rawlings Sporting Goods, USA Today, and the Coca-Cola Company each paid a minimum of $1 million in rights fees plus several millions of dollars more in game day promotions (Macnow, June 26, 1989, 53).

For a company locked out of the top professional sports leagues because of the million dollar plus licensing and promotion costs or because of category exclusivity, there are other alternatives, explains Bob Seagren, a two-time Olympic medalist and sports marketing specialist. "A company can still get in on emerging professional sports, ranging from professional snowmobile racing to arena football, or sponsor any number of grass-roots programs that are gaining in popularity, be they amateur golf tournaments, volleyball tournaments, board sailing competitions, or lacrosse games" (Seagren 1989).

With major brewing companies such as Anheuser-Busch, Inc., and Miller Brewing Company dominating major sports through their sponsorship associations with National Football League teams, major league baseball, college sports, and countless other leagues, it would seem the smaller brewers have no options. But smaller brewers have found a way to connect with their target markets and obtain name exposure, through their sponsorship of "microsports." FX Matt sponsored the Matt's Winter Classic Arm Wrestling Championships. The Sierra Nevada Brewing Company sponsored the Wildflower Classic Century bike ride as well as kayak races and Ultimate Frisbee competitions, while San Francisco Brewing Company sponsored squash tournaments (Johnson 1988, 77).

Marketing through sports strategies encompasses a variety of techniques: sponsoring events, tying in with sports organizations, arranging for celebrity endorsements and personal appearances, capitalizing on appropriate licensing and merchandizing agreements, or owning your own sport and co-promotions.

THE BIG EVENT

To sponsor an event, a company typically will give money to a sports promoter or organizer to create a prize fund. In return, the company can publicize its name through advertising, as well as at the event. Other possible elements of the sponsorship package include acknowledgment in the spectators' programs, opportunities for product exposure or product sampling, a specified number of event tickets, and hospitality tents.

Too often, however, companies that carefully target their television mass media buys wade blithely into event sponsorships with little consideration of some of the most basic marketing questions related to reaching their target market or the specified costs and benefits of sponsorship. Before deciding to sponsor an event, a company must make sure that it fits with the target customer's lifestyle. Skiing, for example, draws the upscale, 35- to 45-year-old age group who buy designer and trendy fashions and sports or luxury cars while tractor pulls and rodeos draw blue-collar fans who purchase jeans, cigarettes, beer, and pickup trucks (Conklin 1986, 30). When Nissan Motor Corporation USA decided to introduce its Infiniti vehicle, it chose to become the official car of the U.S. Open tennis championships and sole sponsor of the men's singles championship. Why? Because the U.S. Open's target audience matched perfectly with the potential Infiniti buyer (Donaton, July 24, 1989, 4). When Cadillac wanted to reach upscale customers, it decided to invest in the Southern California Golf Association's amateur sports tournaments. We helped Cadillac develop the Cadillac Couples Classic program. Cadillac sponsored more than seventy tournaments at some of Southern California's most influential golf clubs. Companies targeting America's aged 55-plus population have sponsored the U.S. National Senior Olympics. A celebration of the health of seniors, the event draws more than four thousand athletes over the age of 55 who compete for medals in cycling, swimming, tennis, track, and pole vaulting. Trans World Airlines, Holiday Inns, and General Foods have been among the sponsors, receiving for their sponsorship fees signage at the games, on-site hospitality tents, category exclusivity, and commercial spots on ESPN (Donaton, June 19, 1989, 12).

Along with image enhancement and product or service exposure opportunities, event sponsorships can be used to build relationships with key clients or as morale builders among employees. As part of their sponsorship, most companies are given hospitality tents, a specified number of free tickets for clients or employees, and VIP seats in the stadium. Miller Brewing Company at the Indianapolis 500 not only sponsored a racing team, but used the event as a launching pad for some corporate hospitality. More than 1,500 corporate clients and guests were entertained at Miller's two hospitality suites (Murphy 1989, 60). At the Kentucky Derby, Coca-Cola was one of several corporations to pay to pitch a tent on the track so that it could bring in its distributors for a pre-Derby party (Kellner 1989, 56). Several years ago, Georgia-Pacific Corporation found its sponsorship of the Atlanta Golf Classic paid off handsomely. The company had been entertaining a Far Eastern executive who played in the tournament, and before he returned home, that executive bought $48 million worth of pulp wood from George-Pacific (Stogel 1988, 27) .

With more than 2,800 companies sponsoring sporting events each year to the tune of some $2.1 billion, according to the Chicago-based Special Events Report (Macnow, June 5, 1989, 53), the risk of sponsorship clutter is ever-present. There are ways around it. A company can buy "title sponsorship," the right to name the event after itself, such as the TWA Frequent Flight Bonus Classic, the Schweppes Challenge, and the Winston Cup Races. If a company decides to sponsor an event, however, it must make sure that it reaches an agreement with the media and not just the event promoters about how the event will be described. When Sunkist Growers decided to sponsor a postseason college football event—the Fiesta Bowl—the company and the game's promoters agreed to have it billed as the "Sunkist Fiesta Bowl." But NBC, which televised the event, continued to call it the Fiesta Bowl, thereby thwarting one of the primary rationales for having title sponsorship—media exposure. American Telephone & Telegraph Company (AT&T) had somewhat better luck by negotiating upfront with CBS to have "tasteful mention" of its AT&T Pebble Beach National Pro Am (Durslag 1987, 18).

Creativity is essential if a company is to stand out from the sponsorship clutter. At an event, officials and workers can wear caps, T-shirts, jackets, and vests featuring a company's logo. If a company is sponsoring track and field events, it can plant its logo on the crossbars from the pole vault or high jump. If a company is sponsoring auto racing, its logo can go on decals of the car. Arranging for on-site exposure of a product is another way to reinforce the connection between a company and the event. When Chrysler Corporation, for example, agreed to sponsor the Triple Crown Challenge in horse racing, it arranged for three Chrysler cars to be parked in the infield of Churchill Downs during the Kentucky Derby, to supply the official cars used on the track, and to provide a new car to the winning jockey, trainer, or owner of the Derby, the Preakness, and Belmont Stakes. Epson America Inc. kept statistics for the PGA tour and scattered its computer systems over several courses so fans could check players' standings. Philip Morris distributed free Marlboro cigarettes at its horse-racing and motor sports sponsorships (Oneal et al. 1987, 50-52).

In event sponsorship, timing is critical. The buildup period before an event may be of equal or greater exposure value than the event itself. If a company supports an Olympic team, for example, it needs to get the message out in the year leading up to the Olympics. Pre-event promotion is vital for all types of sporting events. Well before race day, Miller Brewing Company took a duplicate of its NASCAR entry to shopping centers and other retail outlets, drawing large crowds. The company also sponsored "bathing beauty" contests in local bars before its pro beach volleyball tournament with the runoff held at the event (Oneal et al. 1987, 52). Congratulatory ads or celebrations for teams competing in a sporting event should be planned well in advance. Just as a candidate prepares both an acceptance and concession speech prior to receiving the election results, a company needs to prepare also. The copy for a congratulatory ad, for example, needs to be written weeks before the competition and arrangements made for placement in a particular newspaper or publication the day after the event. When published two weeks after the event, congratulatory ads have little impact.

TEAM SPIRIT

No matter whether it is a U.S. Olympic team or a professional team of bass fisherman—team sponsorship can help a
company reach the heart of its target market on an ongoing,
long-term basis. To appeal to upscale fans, companies such as
Seagram's Glenlivet Scotch and Rolex Watch USA have sponsored a polo team (Fierman 1985, 80). In return, team members
wore jerseys and their mounts sported saddle blankets emblazoned with the corporate name. To appeal to avid fishermen,
Zebco, the makers of a trolling motor and other fishing tackle,
have sponsored a professional team of bass fishermen as well
as a series of tournaments conducted by the Bass Angler's
Sportsman Society (Conklin 1986, 33). The team was outfitted
with clothes carrying the company's emblems. During fish
weigh-ins, the team members were photographed with their
prize-winning fish and the photos were distributed with company press releases.

Amateur as well as professional teams can often suit marketing goals. Going after upscale business executives, BMW of
North America sponsored the Corporate Grand Prix of Skiing,
which involved fifty teams of three executives each.

For a clever marketer, team sponsorship selection can offer
an opportunity to emphasize a product's attributes and points
of distinction. Well-known for its vision care products and accessories, Bausch & Lomb has a natural link with the U.S.
Archery Team, as archery requires superlative eye-hand coor-
dination. Similarly, Subaru's sponsorship of the U.S. Ski Team
enabled the company to emphasize the snow- and ice-handling
capabilities of its four-wheel-drive compact passenger car.

Fan loyalty to the team has translated into substantial new
business for both major corporations and small businesses.
MasterCard increased its business by creating baseball affinity
credit cards which featured individual team logos and entitled
owners to discounts on tickets and team merchandise.

To augment or in place of a team sponsorship, a company
can become involved in team-related promotions. To gain exposure for Rolaids, its antacid tablets, the American Chicle Di-

vision of Warner-Lambert Company established the Rolaids Relief Man Award and then amplified the award through print ads. Anheuser-Busch Inc. tied in its Budweiser brand to the National Hockey League through its promotion of the Budweiser NHL Man of the Year. The hockey teams nominated a candidate based on his sportsmanship and involvement with charitable and civic groups. The winner, selected by a special panel of judges, was named at the Stanley Cup playoffs (McGeehan, March 14, 1988, S-10).

ENDORSEMENTS

Endorsements and personal appearance agreements with current and former celebrity athletes and other sports figures can often deliver both increased market visibility and credibility. Select athletes, many with years of stellar performance in the public limelight, have become the popular embodiment of integrity and excellence—their endorsements are powerful recommendations. Such an athlete is Walter Payton, one of the greatest running backs in National Football League history. Payton was signed by General Mills, Inc. to appear on the front of the Wheaties cereal box; he was the first African-American athlete and one of only five people ever to be featured on the front of the box. We were involved in arranging for that agreement, and I know that General Mills was extremely selective about choosing someone for the cover of the cereal. The athlete had to be a real champion both on and off the field.

Care must be exercised in entering into endorsement agreements. Competitive excellence can only go so far. Of great concern is how the athlete behaves in the public eye. An ounce of bad publicity can undo tons of positive advertising.

In selecting a sports celebrity to do endorsements and public appearances, the standards of conduct expected of senior management apply. It is important to get to know the person well. Are his or her values and standards compatible with the company's? How well does he or she interact with the press? Does he or she have good communication skills and a cooperative attitude? Does he or she have credibility with the target market? Is he or she a Gold Medal winner, a local hero, a nostalgic favorite?

Another element frequently overlooked is the affinity between the product or service and the celebrity. Trans World Airlines' use of Kareem Abdul-Jabbar and Wilt Chamberlain in its commercial to demonstrate the airline's extra legroom was a brilliant approach. Another use of affinity was the commercial that Georgetown University's coach John Thompson did for the Middle Atlantic Milk Marketing Association. The commercial was particularly appropriate, since Thompson was noted for drinking a quart of milk on the sidelines during the games (Comte 1988, 41).

When properly selected and utilized, celebrity endorsements can be a powerful device by which to enter new markets. When Miller Lite launched commercials featuring NFL placekicker Efren Herrera, it earned instant access to the nation's 19.4 million Hispanics. Born in Mexico, Herrera's spectacular college career was at the University of California at Los Angeles, in the heart of the nation's largest Hispanic market. The bulk of Herrera's pro career was in Texas, the second largest Hispanic market.

Athletes are not the only sports figures appropriate for endorsements. Sports heroes, long past their competitive years, coaches, team managers and even family members of big-name athletes have all been among those recruited by businesses. Bruce Jenner, who won an Olympic gold medal for the decathlon in 1976, still appears in endorsements for numerous products. Although dead since 1948, Babe Ruth pitched products for Zenith Electronic Corporation in 1989. In a full-page ad, Zenith showed a picture of Babe Ruth about ready to hit a home run, headlined with the words, "Sometimes a major player can change the whole game." The body of the ad announced that Zenith was now in the power supplies business (Weinstein 1989, 44). Numerous college coaches have lent their names to cereal companies, clothing manufacturers, shoe companies, restaurants, and department stores. Tommy Lasorda, manager of the Los Angeles Dodgers, endorsed Empire of America's Fundbeater Money Market Savings Account in a print ad headlined, "I know a world champion when I see one."

LICENSING AND MERCHANDIZING
AGREEMENTS

Licensing and merchandizing agreements have important functions in today's marketing programs. Licensing is the granting of rights to use a name, logo/trademark, celebrity, or character on products. Emery Worldwide, for example, paid the National Hockey League for the rights to be known as the "official air shipping company," while the Liggett Group, a major tobacco and candy manufacturer, signed a licensing agreement with the National Basketball Association to produce and distribute NBA Hoops cards as the league's official trading cards.

A company must carefully assess whether the properties it seeks match its marketing objectives and whether the dollars it will spend are commensurate with expected results. Time Inc., for instance, paid an estimated $7 million to be the official publisher of the 1988 Olympic Games, but found itself competing with *USA Today*, various Conde Nast publications, and other newspapers and magazines that published special Olympic editions without paying the licensing fee (Konrad 1988, 93). On the other hand, Chrysler Corporation found paying the licensing fee to become the official car and truck of the National Hockey League was worth it. Because hockey was not as heavily sponsored as some other professional sports, Chrysler felt it would not have to fight through commercial clutter. Additionally, the geography of the NHL matched up with where Chrysler has done its best business (McGeehan, March 14, 1988, S-10).

Own Your Own

A decade ago, there were relatively few players in the sports marketing arena. But good ideas have the power of attraction. One way to stand out from the crowd is to own a sport. This ownership is achieved through long-term sponsorship commitment to a specific sport which is supplemented with promotions that position the company as an authority or leader in the sport and that build identification and exposure. All of this does not necessarily require a huge budget. Part of the trick is to identify emerging sports or recreational activities that demographically match the target market. Volvo North America Corporation has made a major run at tennis with not only grassroots amateur and major professional tournaments, but a Volvo Tennis Card that earns discounts for users on the purchase of tennis equipment. Mercedes-Benz of North America has gained a visible predominance in sponsorship of major U.S. urban marathons. If the whole sport is not feasible, a company should carve out a visible niche, as Virginia Slims did with women's tennis.

Guidelines

Virtually all endorsements, team/event sponsorships, and other sports marketing venues need extension, amplification, and resonance in the marketplace. A good ratio to follow is that for every dollar spent on sponsoring fees, an additional $3 should be spent to publicize the connection through advertising campaigns and promotional programs.

Visa amplified the impact of its global Olympic sponsorship with a major print and broadcast advertising effort; with a media tour featuring Olympians Bart Conner (gymnastics), Willie Banks (track and field/triple jump) and Christine Cooper (skiing); and with its Pull for the Team campaign. In that campaign, a percentage of each purchase charged on a Visa card was donated to the U.S. Olympic Committee. Additionally, a toll-free number was established so Visa cardholders could make personal contributions to the U.S. Olympics Committee.

Cadillac Division extended its America's Cup sponsorship of "America II" into prime time television commercials and major magazine spreads. The boat was shown in full spinnaker emblazoned with the Cadillac crest—a commercialism that was not allowed in the actual races.

Point of sale retail displays, sweepstakes, and other grassroots mechanisms can also extend a company's sports marketing investment. When Valvoline Oil Company decided to increase its sales in rural areas, it arranged for its Ashland Oil Inc. subsidiary to sponsor small-town rodeos. The company augmented its exposure at the events by having rodeo-inspired promotions and sweepstakes at local auto parts stores (Oneal et al. 1987, 50).

The network of charitable organizations can be a useful component in obtaining increased publicity and product exposure. Certainly, Georgia-Pacific Corporation, Delta Air Lines Inc., and other official sponsors benefited from the positive publicity associated with the Atlanta Golf Classic. And that publicity came in part because the net proceeds of the event went to Egleston Hospital, a critical-care facility for children (Stogel 1988, 26).

When carefully chosen, the charity can contribute more than the halo effect. It can be an active, rather than passive, partner of the enterprise. The charity's leadership can be networked, and their extensive contacts utilized to aid in the promotion of an event. Frequently, the charity has premiere mailing lists which can serve as major resources for direct mail solicitations in support of both the event and the sponsor's product or service. Additionally, the charity affiliation can be crucial in obtaining the services of athletes who might otherwise reject an endorsement involvement. In Chicago, Walter Payton agreed to become the spokesperson for Energizer Batteries in part because he supported a marketing program which would benefit schools and youth groups in the inner city.

For many companies involved in marketing through sports, co-promotions have enabled them to get much more for their marketing dollars. The types of alliances are limited only by the partners' creativity. In Southern California, Bob's Big Boy Restaurants teamed up with Active West Bowling and Recreation Centers to distribute coupons for three free games of bowling to Bob's patrons who purchased specific menu items. In another coupon promotion, the associate sponsors of the Domino's/Sherson race car team—Domino's Restaurants, Coca-Cola, and Mobil 1 Motor Oil—collaborated on distributing discount coupons for each other's products at Miami area stores during the 1988 CART season (Murphy 1989, 60).

Co-promotions can benefit all participants, regardless of the numbers. We helped orchestrate a co-promotion that involved several hundred players: Reebok International, Life Fitness Inc. (formerly Bally Fitness), Lincoln-Mercury, and some three hundred health and fitness centers across the country. Each health club that purchased Life Fitness Inc.'s Liferower or Life-cycle was entitled to receive Reebok shoes at a special discount price as well a promotion package featuring counter cards, brochures, banners, and sample articles for insertion into club newsletters. For their part, the health clubs awarded free Reebok shoes to any current health club member who recruited a new member. Simultaneously, a sweepstakes program was implemented in which health club members throughout the country could win a Lincoln-Mercury Tracer. Eight Tracers, decorated with Reebok stripes to reinforce the connection, were brought to the health clubs. The program benefited all the players. Life Fitness enhanced its relationship with health centers, the health centers had a promotion that added to their membership rolls, and Lincoln-Mercury had on-site exposure of its Tracer at several hundred health and fitness clubs (*Management Review* 1988, 16).

Contingency Planning

No entry into sports sponsorships should be made without some contingency planning. Sports events and personalities exist within a dynamic environment: parades get cancelled, local athletes win international medals, games get rained out, player strikes occur, winning streaks explode into the headlines, a spokesperson loses in the playoffs. Part of contingency planning is keeping some money in the budget to capitalize on unexpected opportunities or to perform a salvage operation.

Building in some measurable sales elements into the program and tracking system is also important. It is crucial that a company designate someone to oversee a sports buy to see that it gets what it paid for. That person could either be an executive within the organization or a representative affiliated with a sports marketing company.

THE BIG PAYOFFS

Does marketing through sports pay off? Many companies have found it does. Part of the reason that sports marketing is generally effective is that it is a soft sell—a company is not trying to convince its customer to buy a product or service with a standard sales pitch. Instead, it is associating the product or service with something the customer enjoys and to which he or she has an emotional attachment.

Measuring the results of an event or team sponsorship or athlete's endorsement might take some ingenuity, but it can be done. Involvement in the Olympics has been particularly effective in building a company's credibility, according to consumer polls. In 1987, SRI Research Center surveyed 1,000 adults and found that more than half (51 percent) recalled advertising that mentioned a company's status as an Olympic sponsor or supplier, 46 percent said that a company's Olympic sponsorship enhances their opinion of the company, and 37 percent said they would be inclined to buy a product because its manufacturer is an Olympic sponsor (McGeehan, February 1, 1988, 74).

In similar recall studies, Ford Motor Company and Budweiser found that two weeks after a tractor pull they sponsored, 80 percent of those who attended the event could identify them as the sponsors (Conklin 1986, 31).

Other companies have calculated the value of sponsorship by tracking the number of "impressions" it generates and translating that information into an equivalent "worth" in ad dollars. Volvo, for example, found that its $3-million tennis sponsorship in one year generated 1.4-billion impressions, worth about $18 million in advertising (Oneal et al. 1987, 53).

In some cases, sports sponsorships are the only way companies can get television exposure. Cigarette ads are banned from television, but tobacco companies still get exposure for their brands by covering stadiums with their logos during sporting events that are broadcast on television.

Using a dollars and cents measure, Visa concluded that its 1988 Olympic involvement was among its most successful marketing programs in the history of the bank card industry. Substantial increases in charge volume were traced to its Olympic promotions.

Leaf Inc., an Illinois-based candy maker, found that its promotion of selecting honorary batboys and batgirls for games in major and minor league cities, had a positive effect on sales. The promotion was advertised in Sunday newspapers, on packages of Milk Duds and Jolly Rancher candy, and in spectator programs. The entry form had to be accompanied by a UPC symbol found on any Leaf Inc. candy or gum brand. Sales of the affiliated candy brands went up 10 to 15 percent (Macnow, June 26, 1989, 53).

When carefully planned and properly implemented, marketing through sports programs can enhance a company's image, create good community relations, and win the favor of market segments crucial to the company's profitability.

CATCHING THE TIDE

One of my favorite Shakespearean quotes, from *Julius Caesar*—
"There is a tide in the affairs of men, which, taken at the flood
leads on to fortune"—is as relevant today as it was in the six-
teenth century. There are new realities in the marketplace; now
is the time for companies to catch the tide.

Part and parcel of these new realities are some lesser known
but significant consumer segments. They include Asian Americans, the military, gays, and "greens" (environmental activists).

THE ASIAN-AMERICAN MARKET

Asian Americans have been called the "Sleeping Dragon,"
with good reason. At one time, the Asian-American market in
the United States was virtually nonexistent. In 1917, U.S. immigration law put several countries into an "Asiatic Barred
Zone." Asians were not allowed to immigrate to this country.
In fact, it was not until 1952 that Asian countries were given
even token quotas (Bentley 1981, 61). In 1965 Congress eliminated national-origin quotas. Asian immigration now numbers
about 250,000 annually, nearly four times that of European im-

migration and almost equal to that of the Americas. Large numbers of Indochinese refugees, nearly one-half million between 1980 and 1987, have also been allowed into the country since the North Vietnamese took over Saigon in the spring of 1975. A careful look at the statistics reveals that more than half of this nation's Asian Americans arrived after 1970.

The Bureau of the Census lists other "races," mostly Asians, as well as Pacific Islanders, and American Indians, at 8.6 million in population (Waldrop and Exter 1990, 25). Since their numbers are relatively small compared to Hispanics and other minorities, most companies have not included Asian Americans in their marketing efforts. Yet Asian Americans are among this nation's fastest-growing minorities, and they are expected to double in number by the year 2000.

Of even greater importance is their spending power. Asian-American consumers generally outearn the total population, according to a study conducted by Impact Resources, Inc., (1989, i). Furthermore, a higher percentage of Asian Americans than the general population have annual household incomes of $75,000 or more. Even the Indochinese refugees, many of whom have had to exist on welfare as they adjust to their new country, are gradually making their way out of poverty. A federal study found that the longer Indochinese live in the United States, the more fluent they become in English and the more they earn (*Fortune* 1986, 56).

The economic prosperity of many Asians derives in part from the immigrants' dedication to advanced education for themselves and their families, their willingness to form mutual aid societies to help themselves, and their success in operating small businesses.

Among those over the age of 25, nearly one-third (32.9 percent) of Asian Americans have completed four or more years of college, nearly twice the number of whites and four times that of African Americans and Hispanics. Over half (53.3 percent) of all Asians hold managerial or professional positions (Kern 1988, 39).

In 1982, the latest period for which reliable statistics are available, Asian Americans and American Indians owned an estimated 255,642 businesses, generating some $17.9 billion in gross receipts (U.S. Bureau of the Census 1986, 2).

The large concentrations of Asian Americans in California, Hawaii, New York, Illinois, and Texas make these states particularly important for companies wanting to get an early start on reaching the Asian-American market. Although the majority of Asian Americans live in big cities—San Francisco, Los Angeles, New York, Honolulu, Chicago, Houston, Dallas, Washington, D.C., and Seattle—a surprising number have moved to the suburban cities of Southern California. Since 1980, according to a *Los Angeles Times* report (Arax 1987), the number of Asian Americans living in twenty-seven cities and unincorporated areas of the San Gabriel Valley has more than doubled to an estimated 180,000. Monterey Park and adjacent Alhambra are ports of entry for Chinese and other Asians resettling in the United States. Monterey Park now has a 40 percent Asian-American population, the largest of any city in the country, and Alhambra comes close with a 36 percent Asian-American population.

The rapid influx of Asians into the San Gabriel Valley challenged many businesses to adapt or close their doors. Pizza Hut adapted by hiring several Chinese employees to deal with the language and cultural differences (Arax 1987).

Companies that successfully reach the Asian-American market in all part of the United States are those that take time to learn their attitudes, values, and interests. This can be a challenge, since the market is highly fragmented with groups of Chinese, Japanese, Koreans, Filipinos, Indochinese, Pakistanis, Indians, and Iranians all maintaining their relative automony within the larger framework. But there are some lifestyle commonalities. Among them are a traditional respect for one's parents and elders and a propensity to shop in groups. Consumer surveys reveal Asian Americans to be frequent travelers, as well as exercise, sports, and photography enthusiasts (Impact Resources, Inc. 1989, 13). As shoppers, Asian Americans look for quality over price, particularly when buying clothing, electronics equipment, and appliances.

Remy Martin Cognac and Metropolitan Insurance Companies have done well with this consumer segment because they have taken great pains to understand Asian Americans and use marketing and advertising programs that incorporate such key Asian values as quality, security, family, and longevity (Kern 1988, 40). Certainly, this is not an easy task, for it takes an acute awareness of the many social and cultural differences involved. But for those who make the effort, the payoffs could be very great.

THE MILITARY

A somewhat hidden but highly attractive market is the military segment. It reprsents $85 billion in potential buying power and a population of some 9.2 million, more than that of New York City. According to U.S. Department of Defense reports (1988, 23), $34.28 billion is paid annually to active duty military; $26.52 billion is paid to the Department of Defense's civilian employees; $18.73 billion is distributed in pension payments to military retirees; and $5.53 billion is paid to reservists and members of the National Guard. The population of what I call "Military City" is comprised of more than 2.1 million active duty service members, 2.8 million dependents of military personnel, 1.7 million reservists, 1.2 million civilian employees, and 1.4 million military retirees.

Obviously, if a company's target market includes adult males, the military may be an excellent place to find them. About 90 percent of today's active duty military personnel are men aged 18 to 40, and the median age is 24. But it is important to look beyond active duty personnel to their families. Seventy percent of the officers and 51 percent of the enlisted men are married, and among the estimated 2.8 million military dependents are 1.6 million children. On close inspection, it becomes obvious that there is a significant women's segment that needs to be addressed. Consider, for example, the more than 300,000 Navy wives. With their husbands at sea for long periods of time, these women must make most of the day-to-day purchase decisions for the family.

Military families need and want the same things as civilian families. The PX at El Toro Marine Air Station in Orange County,

California, is a case in point. During 1988, the PX did $37 million in sales. Military families and khaki-collared retirees bought all kinds of items, ranging from Benetton sweaters and Oakley sunglasses to Michelin tires and Tandy computers.

The El Toro story is repeated at bases throughout the country. The jointly operated Army and Air Force Exchange Service is now the tenth largest retailer in the nation, chalking up $4.2 billion in sales during 1988. The Marine Corps system, with 18 post exchanges, generated $438 million in sales in 1988 (Takahashi 1989, D-1, 4). These exchanges have changed dramatically from the days when they provided troops with solely necessities such as razors and toilet paper. Today, they carry electronics equipment, sporting goods, small appliances, clothing, health and beauty products, cooking supplies, and food and liquor.

PXs are not only businesses benefiting from the military families' dollars. Real estate, furniture, and appliance businesses surrounding the bases generally do very well catering to the needs of the frequently relocating military families. Fast-food restaurants, pizzerias, and music stores usually do a thriving business because of the prevalence of young adults and children in military towns.

A subsegment of the military community also deserving of attention are the retirees. Although they have decided to hang up their fatigues and draw a government pension, they tend to retire around large military bases where they have ready access to PXs and other services and can remain connected with the military culture and environment. More than one-third of the nation's military retirees live in one of three states. California leads the group with 213,739 retirees, followed by Texas with 142,457 and Florida with 141,487 (Maines 1988, 46). Most military retirees have double-barreled purchasing power, augmenting their military pensions with incomes from second careers, often in sales or marketing.

So how do companies reach these consumers? The military bases are a good starting point. There are some 871 military installations in the 50 states and another 395 in foreign countries and U.S. territories. Some companies advertise in base newspapers, while others sponsor sports and recreational activities. Still others go for the direct one-on-one approach. In Virginia Beach, a real estate company decided to target the military market by creating a family relocation center and training its agents how to sell to military families. It even sent its agents abroad to court military families on their way to the Virginia Beach area (Schwartz 1987, 68). Events sponsored in cities with large concentrations of military families, such as San Diego, California, and Norfolk, Virginia, can also serve as an entree into the military market.

GAYS

While talking about "gays" as a consumer segment is highly controversial and may make company executives and shareholders somewhat uncomfortable, it is important to acknowledge that the market exists and has a substantial amount of economic clout. There are an estimated 8 to 10 million gay men in the United States.

Because, for the most part, they do not have families to raise, they generally have more discretionary income than the general population. Results of surveys conducted by Simmons Market Research Bureau and the *Advocate*, a news and feature magazine for gay men and lesbians, showed that *Advocate* readers were both well educated and affluent (*American Demographics* 1988, 20). An estimated 61 percent were college graduates, many with advanced degrees; 95 percent were employed; 64 percent had professional or managerial positions; and their average household income was $47,800.

Many gays have come to think of themselves as a kind of ethnic group. Werner Kuhn, executive director of the Gay and Lesbian Community Center of Orange County, California, explains that gays are often treated unfairly. "For that reason they bind together and share the same feelings of brotherhood and sisterhood that people of other cultures share" (Erwin 1989, B-1).

To address the market directly, a company could advertise in publications with a high gay readership or have a discrete presence at events, such as the Lesbian and Gay Pride Weekend in New York and the Orange County Cultural Pride Festival. Indirectly, gays can be reached through sponsorship of the arts, support of AIDS fund-raisers, or sponsorship of community events in cities where gays tend to live, such as San Francisco and Laguna Beach, California.

THE COMING OF THE GREENS

Three out of four Americans (76 percent) identify themselves as "environmentalists," and 41 percent say they are strong environmentalists, according to a Gallup poll (Kohut and Shriver 1989).

The environment as an issue of public concern "has moved from the marshes to the mainstream," according to Jay Hair, president and chief executive officer of the National Wildlife Federation (1989B, 29). Symbolic of the movement of environmental issues to the top of the nation's political, social, and economic agenda is *Time* magazine's January 2, 1989, cover which named Endangered Earth as "Planet of the Year" and its January 15, 1990 cover on "Antarctica—Is Any Place Safe From Mankind?"

The environmental fervor is being fanned by reactions to the Alaskan oil spill; by concerns about pollution, loss of natural habitats for wildlife, acid rain, global warming, deforestation, and depletion of the ozone layer; by fears about hazardous and radioactive waste and radon gas; and by anxieties about carcinogenic pesticides.

Environmental activists (or "greens" as they have been named) are not only starting recycling centers and car pools, but they are also forming their own political party. Spurred by European environmentalists who have organized political parties and won some elections, many U.S. environmentalists met at the second national Green Gathering in Oregon in June 1989 to develop political platforms. Their goal was to create a viable third political party in the United States. The influence of the greens is already reaching the political mainstream. New York City, for instance, passed a law banning the manufacturing of styrofoam (styrofoam contains chloroflurocarbons which deplete the earth's ozone layer), and President George Bush promised to convene a Global Environmental Summit (*Windstar Journal* 1989, 31, 55).

Coming from many backgrounds, the greens include scientists and artists, engineers and entrepreneurs, ex-flower children and New Left activists. But their common bond is their commitment to create a sustainable future, one in which humankind is in partnership with nature. They perceive the earth as a living organism, with humankind part of that organism.

On a less philosophical note, the environmental movement is a natural outgrowth of the health and fitness consciousness of many Americans. When exercise walking or doing aerobics, people do not want to be worse off because they have inhaled physical impurities in the air. If people are encouraging their children to eat fruits and vegetables instead of junk food, they want to feel confident that the produce does not contain pesticides.

Environmental issues have expanded over the years from the arenas of public relations and political activism to the marketplace. More and more, corporations are being called to task because of their actions on ecological issues. Already, the Council on Economic Priorities has published a resource booklet entitled "Shopping for a Better World," which rates many companies by their conduct on global issues, including their pesticide use and illegal dumping (*Windstar Journal* 1989, 56). The Center for Science in the Public Interest published a list of more than one hundred sources of organically produced fruits, vegetables, grains, and meats (Silberner 1989, 59). In one survey, 47 percent of all consumers, and 57 percent of those with household incomes of $50,000 or more, have changed their purchase behavior because of environmental concerns. Sixty-one percent of all consumers are more inclined to go to a store or restaurant that is committed to reducing its use of plastic containers and utensils (Russell 1989, 2). In the Gallup poll cited earlier, three out of four Americans said they have taken steps to improve the quality of the environment, and nearly one out of every three (29 percent) said they have boycotted a company's products because of its record on the environment.

What is happening in Europe is likely to be a precursor to what will happen here. Throughout the European Economic

Community, sales of unleaded gasoline, recycled paper, "ozone friendly" aerosols, and biodegradable diapers are soaring, according to a *U.S. News & World Report* article (Knight and Dimmler 1989, 46). Additionally, whole new industries are emanating from pollution control efforts. Some nine thousand European firms employing more than one million workers are involved in everything from the production of catalytic converters for cars to waste-disposal technology. It has become a $35-billion-a-year business.

In the United States, retailers are beginning to respond to the environmental concerns of their customers by making room on their shelves for biodegradable paper products, "all natural" baby food products, pump rather than aerosol dispensers, organically grown fruits and vegetables, recycled paper, and many other "environmental friendly" products. Many manufacturers are also responding by redesigning products, changing their packaging, and telling the public through their ads and commercials what they are doing right. Environmental appeals are showing up in marketing messages. A selling point for a refrigerator is that it is "energy efficient." An investment company runs a print ad touting the 1990s as "The Decade of Environmental Action" and inviting readers to invest in the Freedom Environment Fund (*Orange County Register* 1989, C-8).

Among the many steps businesses can take to reach environmentalists might be supporting and working with environmental organizations, such as the National Wildlife Federation, Nature Conservancy, Sierra Club, American Cetacean Society, Environmental Defense Fund, and Windstar Foundation. The National Wildlife Federation alone has 4.8 million members. In the Gallup poll mentioned earlier, 49 percent of the Americans surveyed said they contributed money to an environmental, conservation, or wildlife preservation group, and one out of six said they had done volunteer work for such a group. Some corporations are already working cooperatively with environmental organizations. Weyerhaeuser Company, USX Corporation, and 3M are among the corporate members of the National Wildlife Federation's Corporate Conservation Council. The council has issued a number of policy statements on topics ranging from wetlands protection to soil erosion to waste reduction. It has also honored several businesses that have made outstanding achievements in the area of conservation (Hair 1989A, 27, 28). Companies working in cooperation with rather than in opposition to environmental groups will earn the respect of the greens and consumers in general. Such companies are demonstrating social responsibility and a recognition that this nation's natural resources represent the capital that will "finance" our future economic growth and well-being.

REGIONAL MARKETING

As corporate America reexamines mass marketing, regional marketing has for many companies become a practical way to win and keep vital markets. *American Demographics* editor Brad Edmondson describes regional marketing as the "next stage of market segmentation—another way for large companies to scatter themselves into the countless niches created by individualistic American consumers" (1988, 25).

Regional marketing involves dividing the country into well-defined geographic regions, such as the Southwest or East Coast, or into so-called "vernacular" regions. Vernacular regions are those perceived to exist by their inhabitants and other members of the population at large, such as the Bible Belt, Kentucky Bluegrass Country, and New England (Zelinsky 1989, 43). The point is that within these geographic or vernacular regions, the inhabitants often share socioeconomic and lifestyle characteristics that set them apart from other areas. These may include income and educational levels, religious attitudes and practices, political outlooks, speech patterns, product preferences, manner of dress, music, traditions, symbols, and history. In buying power alone, there are sharp differences. For example, the median family income for Northeasterners was $33,940 in 1987, compared to $28,250 for Southerners (U.S. Bureau of the Census 1988, 3). There are also major differences in the sales for many products when analyzed by region. Californians like BMWs, Mercedes-Benzes, and other luxury imported cars, while many Southwesterns prefer pickup trucks. Cream cheese and waffles tend to sell better in the Northeast, Japanese food and soy sauce sell better in the Northwest, and cake mixes and cottage cheese sell better in the Midwest and mountain states (Schiffman and Kanuk 1987, 59). Even when the product is the same, there can be regional differences. Ford Motor Company's designers found that in Los Angeles and other parts of the West, consumers prefer their sports cars white, followed by black and red, whereas Midwesterners choose black, followed by red and white (Curtindale 1989, 56). When it comes to pickles, Northwesterners prefer theirs very sour compared to the rest of the U.S. population (Moore 1985, 68).

Some geographic areas merit attention because of their economic strength and pervasive influence. California has one of the largest Gross National Products in the world. Stephen Levy, an economist, points out that because of its diversified economy the "Golden State" will account for one-fifth of the U.S. economic growth in the coming years. Already the most ethnically diverse market in the nation, California will become even more so in the 1990s (Riche 1989, 8). John Naisbitt characterizes California as the "bellwether state," pointing out that it is the home of the "granola ethic," the human potential movement, and the physical fitness trend (1984, xxvii). Perhaps the state's trend-setting influence explains why so many corporations are bringing their marketing managers and design firms to California. All of the Big Three domestic automakers, for instance, have opened design studios in California (Shriver 1990, D-1).

One of the pioneers in regional marketing is Campbell Soup Company. It saw regional marketing as a way to find new market niches and ultimately increase total sales. As part of its regional strategy, Campbell cooked up some new products and substantially revamped its marketing efforts. It was appropriately rewarded for its efforts. When its pork and beans did not sell well in the Southwest compared to a local competitor's product, the company deleted the pork and added some chili pepper, thereby creating ranchero beans. Its sales of pinto beans in the Southwest went from virtually nothing to 75,000 cases in 1984 (Moore 1985, 68).

Other important corporations also have entered the regional arena. Miller Brewing Company had actor Randy Quaid, a Texas native, appear in its regional advertising campaign based on

Texas history. The campaign capitalized on the fact that Texans have a strong identification with the Lone Star state and that they are required to learn about the Alamo and other aspects of the state's history in their schools.

Levi Strauss & Company also developed a regional flavor in its Levi's 501 U.S.A. Jeans campaign. The campaign took a carefully targeted look at young people in eight different parts of the country, ranging from Cape Ann, Massachusetts, to Antelope Valley, California. One of major themes in the campaign was that the youth valued their local roots and friends and were not anxious to leave (Lippert 1989, 18).

How do companies put local flavor into their marketing? Campbell relied on its regional sales managers to create regional and local promotions. The brand sales manager in Pittsburgh, for instance, created a joint promotion with a television station and a local auto dealer. For one week, Campbell products and the auto dealer received free advertising in return for a carload of Campbell products given away at the end of the week. In California, Campbell Soup and a local ski resort teamed up to reduce the price of lift tickets in return for Campbell Soup labels (Carpenter 1987, 44). In its regional approach, Miller used local heroes as spokespersons. Carmakers, such as Chrysler Corporation, film their ads in terrain that matches the market. Arby's Roast Beef Restaurants delivered messages with different audio "tags" so that local restaurants could advertise specialized products, such as fish sandwiches during Lent for the Northeast market (Edmondsom 1988, 26).

The benefits of regional marketing are many. An executive of Campbell Soup contends that it makes a company more competitive by forcing it to think like its local competitors and enabling it to compete in areas it might never have considered before (Carpenter 1987, 45). For companies in mature or declining markets, regionalization can translate into growth opportunities. S. C. Johnson & Son, maker of Raid, increased its market share in sixteen out of eighteen regions and its overall market share by 5 percent by adopting a regional marketing strategy that promoted flea sprays in the South and cockroach insecticides in New York (Moore 1985, 68).

CHANGES

Along with monitoring emerging consumer segments, a company must also consider the societal, economic, and political changes likely to occur in the 1990s and beyond. All of these changes will dramatically impact the marketing environment.

Communication

What Alvin Toffler described in the *Third Wave* as the demassification of media will continue and intensify (1980, 158). With the advent of desktop publishing and high-quality copying machines, even a small business can produce a newsletter or magazine.

The speed by which we can communicate over long distances has become faster and more efficient. As a result, styles and fashions which once took months and years to reach from one country to another, now take hours. People in Kansas who have satellite dishes see clothing styles not only from the United States but from Paris.

Cocooning

Cocooning is an exceedingly important trend. With the advent of affordable personal computers and modems, facsimile machines, copiers, and improved telephone technology, some 27 million people have now elected to work out of their homes. One-third of all new businesses registered in 1988 were operated out of the home. Additionally, a Roper poll found that 44 percent of Americans think they might like to try working at home. Only 27 percent said they would never give up the office (Tooley and Woltz 1988, 121).

Cocooning presents some major challenges to marketers. It affects not only how we live, but where we live. Since it may no longer be necessary to live within easy commuting distance of corporate offices, many home business workers have moved further away from mainstream markets into small towns. How does a company reach a commodities broker who works out of his home via computer or a magazine writer who develops articles through telephone interviews and sends them to magazine editors via modem? Certainly, direct mail is an option, but it can be very expensive and the message can get lost in the clutter. Businesses must look at alternative marketing approaches. Such approaches might include Shopper's Advantage, a discount shopping club accessible through one's personal computer, or the Home Shopping Network via television.

Cultural Events

Cultural events and the arts in general will become major competitors for recreational and leisure dollars in America. In 1988, the number of people attending cultural events (plays, concerts, museum exhibits) exceeded the number of people attending sporting events. The "graying of America" is one reason for this trend. The median age of the U.S. population is rising. As people age they attend more cultural events. In a study conducted by the Daniel Yankelovich Group, Inc. (1987, 13), researchers found that among Americans aged 39 to 49, 24 percent gave high priority to cultural enrichment, such as going to concerts and museums, compared to 25 percent who gave high priority to attending sports events. Among those 50 years and older, 24 percent gave high priority to attending cultural events and 21 percent to sports events. Philip Morris, in its involvement with the American Business Committee for the Arts, Inc. serves as an excellent model for other corporations to follow.

Corporations as Allies

Corporations are becoming allies in people's lives, particularly in the areas of parenting, health, and education. To meet the needs of dual career and single parents, corporations are establishing child-care consultation and referral programs, on-site child-care centers, job sharing, and flexible work hours. These fringe benefits become key issues in employee recruitment and retention.

Faced with ever-rising health care costs for their employees, progressive businesses are also taking a renewed interest in keeping their employees well and in detecting life-threatening health problems early. Exercise rooms, health club memberships, and health screenings are all part of the new thrust toward employee health, and these opportunities are readily presented as employee perks.

The shortage of well-educated competent employees has prompted American businesses to spend an estimated $30 billion in 1988 on training, retraining, and educating their employees (Long 1988, 40). Many companies are financially assisting employees who want to start or complete college degrees, while others are holding a variety of on-site seminars and classes, such as English classes for immigrants. Still others are entering into partnership programs with area schools to help improve basic math and reading skills. Businesses need to reexamine their support of public and private education. They can pay for education in the schools now, or they can pay for it later on the job.

Power to the Minorities

Europeans—Irish, Italians, Russian Jews, and German Jews—invented ethnic politics and then used that power base to improve their economic lots. There will be a similar increase in political militancy on the part of African Americans, Hispanics, and other minority groups. By the year 2000, African Americans and Hispanics will constitute a decided majority in nearly one-third of the nation's fifty largest cities. This is bound to spur radical changes. What some of those changes could be and how they might affect businesses was highlighted in an *EBONY* article entitled, "The Biggest Secret of Race Relations: The New White Minority" (1989, 88). "If blacks are indeed going to become the new majorities in cities like Oakland, Atlanta and Chicago, then economic empowerment—as well as political empowerment—is within reach," the article says. "As a sizeable portion of the consumer market . . . blacks can leverage concessions from manufacturers, retailers, developers and financial institutions to invest in the cities, bringing jobs, affordable housing, and quality education." Hispanics, too, have come a long way politically since the days when Cesar Chavez organized the farm workers' strike. They are gaining mainstream political posts as mayors, congressional representatives, and state officials. With Hispanics continuing to organize politically, the stage is set for them to organize economically as well.

As minority groups organize, it is likely that they will increasingly rely on economic boycotts to make their point. And it will not be just Hispanics and African Americans. When Continental Airlines ran a television campaign showing a samurai warrior slashing high airfares, the Chinese for Affirmative Action labeled the campaign "racist." After being threatened with a boycott, Continental pulled the spots in Seattle and Spokane, Washington (Teinowitz 1989, 3). More and more, companies must consider the sensitivities of minority groups. Their bottom lines may depend on it.

Fitting into a Global Economy

After World War II, the United States was an undisputed industrial leader in the world. But the reality is that U.S. companies no longer dominate world markets and have intense competition, even on the homefront. Traditional calls to market patriotism, such as "Buy American" campaigns, seldom sell a company's product or service. Americans purchase goods and services that meet their interests, needs, and budgets, and they frequently could care less about where they come from. The free market is likely to increase, and a company may discover that its next corporate competitor is in Hong Kong or an economically liberated Eastern Bloc nation. On the other hand, the opportunities continue to exist for companies to take their products and services abroad. Segmentation, by its emphasis on understanding and adapting to differences, will serve businesses well. Both U.S. cigarette and soup companies, for example, have discovered that taste preferences in the United Kingdom do not parallel those of U.S. consumers (Schiffman and Kanuk, May 1987, 61) and have changed some products. Experts in marketing to Eastern Europe and the Soviet Union explain that entrepreneurs "will make a foothold in Moscow or Warsaw or Prague if they're able to go in knowing the culture, being sensitive to business practices and being flexible in negotiations" (Harrell and Armstrong 1989, D-4).

BEING PREPARED

To respond to challenges ahead, American businesses need to make some changes in both their marketing and sales departments and in their marketing strategies. It is a wise corporation that hires its marketing people as a reflection of the diversity of the marketplace. If a company's marketing executives come from elite, insulated, intellectual environments then their thinking is likely to reflect that bias. It makes no sense to develop marketing programs directed at Hispanics without Hispanic employees being part of the process. One of our company's strengths is that we have diversity coupled with open communication. Quite often, our Hispanic, college, or women's marketing experts will keep us on track and contribute new dimensions to our marketing strategies that many times prove to be the critical difference in a campaign's success.

That corporations can benefit from the plethora of research information being generated on consumer markets there is no doubt. Consider the data available from just the use of scanner cash registers, people meters, panel diaries, market research reports, and U.S. census reports and data tapes. Not only will marketers have to be extraordinarily skilled at processing vast amounts of information and making sense out of it, they will have to be much more. What is needed are marketers who can use touch, feeling, and intuition to creatively apply all this information and data to very specific consumer markets. What is required is hard work, understanding, empathy, and a commitment to the marketplace.

Corporations can no longer afford to market from afar. Product technology is advancing so rapidly that there is little difference between most products. How consumers feel about a product becomes more and more important. A company must foster an affinity toward itself and its product.

If I am able to leave business leaders with but one message from these chapters it is to skip the stopover cocktail in Chicago and visit the Hispanic communities there; have lunch on a nearby university campus; go to an urban gospel concert; reconsider Greenwich Village as a market; visit a military base; and attend the Senior Olympics. Get out and meet the members of the company's target segments, observe them, become an integral part of their lives, build ongoing relationships. In that way, you can feel and adapt to the pace of change. The marketplace is dynamic! If you do not get into the game and become a committed player, not only are you likely to lose the match, but the entire ballpark can walk away from you.

REFERENCES

INTRODUCTION

Naisbitt, John. 1984. *Megatrends*. New York: Warner.
Nielsen Media Research. 1988. *Nielsen 1988 report on television*. Northbrook, Ill.: A. C. Nielsen.
Peters, Tom. 1988. *Thriving on chaos, handbook for a management revolution*. New York: Knopf.
Smith, Page. 1985. *American enters the world—a people's history of the progressive era and World War I*. Vol. 7. New York: McGraw-Hill.

CHAPTER 1. SEGMENTATION AND THE LIFESTYLE APPROACH

Business Committee for the Arts, Inc. November 1986. *Involving the arts in marketing: a business strategy*. New York: Business Committee for the Arts, Inc.
College Stores Research and Educational Foundation. October 23, 1986. Student Watch 86, college consumer survey. Press release—nation's first comprehensive college consumer survey reveals what students think, what they buy, what they spend and where.
Forbes. August 26, 1985. Rifle shot marketing.
Kotkin, Joel. July 1987. Selling to the new America. *Inc*.

Lazarus, George. 1988. *Marketing immunity—Breaking Through Customer Resistance*. Homewood, Ill.: Dow Jones-Irwin.

Marketing News. July 31, 1987. Marketing's role, function to narrow: Editors' panel.

Martinez, Angel. November 1988. Reebok sprinting ahead through influence marketing. *Management Review*. Also: Personal interview, June 29, 1988.

McLaughlin, Steven D., and Denise M. Zimmerle. 1988. *The Cosmopolitan report, part three—the changing life course of American women consumer behavior*. New York: Hearst Corp. (prepared by Battelle Human Affairs Research Centers in Seattle, Washington).

Rapp, Stan and Thomas L. Collins. 1989. *MaxiMarketing*. New York: New American Library.

Shiver, Jube, Jr. June 22, 1989. Surveys find black customers represent vast profit potential. *Los Angeles Times*.

Smith, Martin J. November 15, 1988. The political truth. *Orange County Register*.

Smith, Wendell R. July 1956. Product differentiation and market segmentation of alternative marketing strategies. *Journal of Marketing*.

Strategy Research Corp. April 13, 1989. 1989 U.S. Hispanic market study highlights domestic market expansion (press release). Los Angeles, Calif.: Strategy Research.

Toffler, Alvin. 1980. *The third wave*. New York: William Morrow.

Westerman, Marty. March, 1989. Death of the Frito bandito. *American Demographics*.

CHAPTER 2. GETTING THERE FROM HERE

Lazarus, George. 1988. *Marketing immunity—breaking through customer resistance*. Homewood, Ill.: Dow Jones-Irwin.

Levitt, Theodore, 1986. *The marketing imagination*. New York: Free Press.

Lieblich, Julia. November 21, 1988. If you want a big new market. *Fortune*.

CHAPTER 3. SECURE ADULTS

AARP (American Association of Retired Persons). 1988. *A Profile of Older Americans*. Long Beach, Calif.: American Association of Retired Persons.

Alsop, Ronald and Bill Abrams. 1986. *The Wall Street Journal on marketing*. Homewood, Ill.: Dow Jones-Irwin.

Berlow, Ellen. April 22, 1988. The booming business of aging. *Washington Post*.

Cain, Carol. October 21, 1988. Older Americans don't feel their age. *Detroit News*.

Center for Mature Studies. 1988. *Consumer behavior of older adults—a national survey*. Atlanta, Ga.: Georgia State University.

Chipkin, Harvey. March 16, 1987. Senior citizens grow up—as one of the hottest aviation markets. *Travel Weekly*.

Cortez, Susana. March 13, 1989. Telephone interview.

Daniel Yankelovich Group, Inc. Fall 1987, *The mature Americans—a study of today's men and women 50 years and over*.

Dychtwald, Ken. 1989. *Age wave*. Los Angeles, Calif.: Jeremy P. Tarcher.

Edmondson, Brad. November 1986. Who gives to charity. *American Demographics*.

———. June 1987. Is Florida our future? *American Demographics*.

———. November 1987. Inside the empty nest. *American Demographics*.

Friedman, Peter. February 27, 1989. Telephone interview.

Koenig, Helena. March 10, 1989. Telephone interview.

Nielsen Media Research. 1988. *Nielsen 1988 report on television*. Northbrook, Ill.: A. C. Nielsen.

Robinson, John P. March 1987. Where's the boom. *American Demographics*.

Rosenfeld, Jeffrey P. January 1986. Demographics on vacation. *American Demographics*.

Schwartz, Jim, and Jim Stone. April 1987. New-car buyers. *American Demographics*.

Senior World/Orange County. February 1989. Classified advertising-solo seniors.

Senior World/Orange County. June 1986. Eunice finds joy in helping others.

Sporting Goods Business. May 1988. Seniors spent most on golf in 1987.

U.S. Bureau of the Census. July 1986. Current population reports series P-70, no. 7. *Household Wealth and Asset Ownership: 1984*. Washington, D.C.: U.S. Government Printing Office.

U.S. Travel Data Center. 1989. Interview.

Wolfe, David B. July 1987. The ageless market. *American Demographics*.

CHAPTER 4. WOMEN

Alsop, Ronald, and Bill Abrams. 1986. *The Wall Street Journal on marketing*. Homewood, Ill.: Dow Jones-Irwin.

American Council on Education/University of California, Los Angeles. 1988. Freshman participation in federal student aid programs continues to decline; telephone interview with Ellyne Berz. 1988 freshman survey results.

Battaglia, Beverly A. July 1989. Breaking the glass ceiling. *Business to Business*.

Bonker, Dawn. July 20, 1989. Do children benefit from having older parents? *Orange County Register*.

Cleaver, Joanne Y. March 7, 1988. Lifestyle ads boost banks, insurers. *Advertising Age*.

Cook, Suzanne D. June 2, 1988. How to tap the women's market of the '90s. *American Demographics Instant Replay Seminar Series*.

Curtindale, Frieda. November 1988. Marketing cars to women. *American Demographics*.

Deitrich, Don. August 15, 1989. Telephone interview.

Doyle, Thomas B. May 1989. Survival of the fittest. *American Demographics*.

Evans, Joni. April 1989. Joy riding. *Vogue*.

Folse, Lynn. September 12, 1985. Workers labor to raise women's status. *Advertising Age*.

Gonzales, Monica. January 1988. The women's card. *American Demographics*.

———. March 1988. Cosmo's crystal ball. *American Demographics*.

Haynes, Kevin. January 1987. Hey, big spender. *Working Woman*.

Johnston, William B., and Arnold E. Packer. June 1987. *Workforce 2000— Work and Workers for the Twenty-first Century*. Indianapolis Ind.: Hudson Institute.

Ladies Home Journal. May 1988. Have women's lives really changed?

Martinez, Angel. November 1988. Two CEO-driven improvement programs. *Management Review*.

McLaughlin, Steven D., and Denise M. Zimmerle. 1988. *The Cosmopolitan report, part three—the changing life course of American women consumer behavior*. New York: Hearst Corp. (prepared by Battelle Human Affairs Research Centers in Seattle, Wash.).

Mendelsohn, Frances D. August 1987. When retailers patronize women, women won't patronize their stores. *PC Week*.

Profit Building Strategies for Business Owners. October 1988. Stores that traditionally appeal to men are making a pitch to women. .

Russell, Cheryl. January 1989. Not waiting around. *American Demographics.*

Selinger, Iris Cohen. December 1986. Staying power. *Madison Avenue.*

Sonenklar, Carol. June 1986. Women and their magazines. *American Demographics.*

Steinberg, Janice. March 7, 1988. Signs point to great reach via outdoors. *Advertising Age.*

U.S. Bureau of the Census. April 1986. *1982 economic censuses: Women-owned businesses.* Washington, D.C.: U.S. Government Printing Office.

———. February 1989. current population reports series P-609, no. 162. *Money Income of Households, Families and Persons in the United States: 1987.* Washington, D.C.: U.S. Government Printing Office.

U.S. Bureau of Labor Statistics. January 1989. *Employment and Earnings.* Washington, D.C.: U.S. Government Printing Office.

———. August 3, 1989. Unpublished data.

———. Women's Bureau. August 15, 1989. Telephone interview with Mike Williams.

Vogue. April 1989.

Wallis, Claudia. December 4, 1989. Onward, Women! *Time.*

CHAPTER 5. COLLEGE STUDENTS

Advertising Age. February 6, 1989. National college media use chart from the Simmons Market Research Bureau study of College Market Publications, 1988.

American Council on Education/University of California, Los Angeles. 1986. New report tracks 20 year shift in freshman attitudes, values and life goals.

———. 1989. Freshman participation in federal student aid programs continues to decline; telephone interview with Ellyne Berz. 1988 freshman survey results.

Chronicle of Higher Education. April 1988.

College Stores Research and Educational Foundation. 1986. Student Watch 86, college consumer survey. Brochure.

———. October 23, 1986. Student Watch 86, college consumer survey. Press release—nation's first comprehensive college consumer survey reveals what students think, what they buy, what they spend and where.

Fecht, Gerald. October 1989. Personal interview.

Finn, Chester E. January 27, 1988. U.S. campuses are bursting at the quads. *Wall Street Journal*.

Graham, Lawrence, and Lawrence Hamdan. 1987. *Capturing the $160 billion youth market*. New York: St. Martin's.

Hughes, Veronica. September 1988. Fraternities and sororities now. *College Store Journal*.

Lipman, Joanne. March 21, 1989. Spring break sponsors in Florida find too much of a good thing. *Wall Street Journal*.

Serafin, Raymond. February 2, 1987. Pickups deliver a ton of first-time buyers. *Advertising Age*.

Sherer, Jill. February 6, 1989. Media watch. *Advertising Age*.

Sherrid, Pamela and Linda K. Lanier. May 5, 1986. Ringing the cash register on campus. *U.S. News & World Report*.

Simmons Market Research Bureau, Inc. 1985.

Steinberg, Janice. February 1, 1988. Samples as abundant as sunshine. *Advertising Age*.

———. February 1, 1988. Sampling often worth years of loyalty. *Advertising Age*.

———. February 6, 1989. Media 101. *Advertising Age*.

U.S. Bureau of the Census. August 1988. Current population reports, series P-20, no. 429. *School Enrollment—Social and Economic Characteristics of Students: October, 1986*. Washington, D.C.: U.S. Government Printing Office.

———. February 1989. Current population reports, series P-60, no. 162. *Money Income of Households, Families and Persons in the United States: 1987*. Washington, D.C.: U.S. Government Printing Office.

Vakil, Jayshree. February 6, 1989. What is the biggest myth about the college market. *Advertising Age*.

Weinstein, Fannie. February 1, 1988. Time to get them in your franchise. *Advertising Age*.

CHAPTER 6. HISPANICS

Arce, Carlos. June 3, 1987. How to reach the Hispanic market. *American Demographics Instant Replay Seminar Series*.

Barber, Ben. October 30, 1988. Hispanic purchasing power attracts corporate attention. *Blade* (Toledo, Ohio).

Cuneo, Alice Z. February 13, 1989. Hills Bros. push percolates from bottom to top. *Advertising Age*.

Edel, Richard. February 13, 1989. Future seen in P & G's well-oiled machine. *Advertising Age*.

Elizalde, Hector. June 3, 1987. How to reach the Hispanic market. *American Demographics Instant Replay Seminar Series*.

Feuer, Jack. February 20, 1989 Hispanic youth and TV: Tuning in two cultures. *Adweek*.

Freeman, Laurie. February 8, 1988. As events grow, so does skepticism. *Advertising Age*.

Hansen, Laurie. September 23, 1988. Church here 50% Hispanic. *Tidings*.

Kemp, Bernie. May 5, 1989. Telephone interview.

Lacayo, Richard. July 11, 1988. A surging new spirit. *Time*.

Lopez, Ruben. June 3, 1987. How to reach the Hispanic market. *American Demographics Instant Replay Seminar Series*.

Marasca, Alfred. August 1989. Personal interview.

Marz, Pablo. July 28, 1989. Telephone interview.

McCarthy, K., and R. B. Valdez. May 1986. *Current and future effects of Mexican immigration in California*. Santa Monica, Calif.: RAND Corp.

Rodriguez, Richard. July 11, 1988. The fear of losing a culture. *Time*.

Schwartz, Joe. February 1989. Frito parks. *American Demographics*.

Stroud, Ruth. February 13, 1989. GTE leaves its bill stuffing days behind. *Advertising Age*.

Strategy Research Corp. 1984. *U.S. Hispanic market study*. New York: Strategy Research.

———. 1986. *1987 U.S. Hispanic market study*. New York: Strategy Research.

———. April 13, 1989. 1989 U.S. Hispanic market study highlights domestic market expansion (press release). Los Angeles, Calif.: Strategy Research.

U.S. Bureau of the Census. August 1988(A). Current population reports, series P-60, no. 161. *Money Income and Poverty Status in the United States: 1987*. (Advance data from the March 1988 current population survey.) Washington, D.C.: U.S. Government Printing Office.

———. August 1988(B). *The Hispanic population in the United States: March, 1988*. (Advance report.) Washington, D.C.: U.S. Government Printing Office.

———. February 1989. Current population reports, series P-60, no. 162. *Money Income of Households, Families and Persons in the United*

States: 1987. Washington, D.C.: U.S. Government Printing Office.

Veciana-Suarez, Ana. 1987. *Hispanic media, USA.* Washington, D.C.: Media Institute.

Volkman, Ilona. 1989. Telephone interview.

Weinstein, Bob. February 13, 1989. Undeveloped market exposed. *Advertising Age.*

Zapata, Carman. July 28, 1989. Telephone interview.

CHAPTER 7. AFRICAN AMERICANS

Barras, Jonetta Rose. June 1989. Afro-American art and the corporate dollar. *American Visions.*

———. June 1989. The arts—and more. *American Visions.*

Bennett, Claudette. June 1, 1988. Emerging opportunities in ethnic markets. *American Demographics Instant Replay Series.*

Bennett, Lerone, Jr. August 1986. The 10 biggest myths about the black family. *EBONY.*

Cruse, Harold. 1987. *Plural but equal.* New York: William Morrow.

EBONY August 1986. Black love and the extended family concept should be priorities.

———. August 1988. What must be done.

———. October 1988. Rich black $, rich white $: Are they different?

———. May 1989. Backstage.

———. May 1989. Who's hot, who's not in 1989 (second annual readers' poll).

Gadsden, Sheila. September 12, 1985. Seeking the right track in talking to blacks. *Advertising Age.*

Jackson, Jesse L. February 1989. *Harper's Bazaar.*

Jet. March 6, 1989. Coca-Cola USA to award $130,000 in scholarships.

Miller, Mark. February 13, 1989. A new tobacco alliance; the smoking industry looks to blacks for support. *Newsweek.*

Olson, Carin. January 13, 1989. Health educators turn to black community's leaders, organizations, other strengths. *JAMA: The Journal of the American Medical Association.*

Pfaff, Fred, and Rebecca Fannin. March 1986. Media with a mission. *Marketing and Media Decisions.*

Poinsett, Alex. August 1988. Suffer the little children. *EBONY.*

Schwartz,, Joe. January 1989. Black clout. *American Demographics.*

Shiver, Jube, Jr. June 22, 1989. Surveys find black customers represent vast profit potential. *Los Angeles Times.*

U.S. Bureau of the Census. March 1988. Current population reports, series P-25, no. 1022. *United States Population Estimates, by Age, Sex, and Race: 1980 to 1987*. Washington, D.C.: U.S. Government Printing Office.

———. February 1989. Current population reports, series P-60, no. 162. *Money Income of Households, Families and Persons in the United States: 1987*. Washington, D.C.: U.S. Government Printing Office.

———. January 1989. Current population reports, series P-25, no. 1018. *Projections of the Population of the United States, by Age, Sex and Race: 1988 to 2080*. Washington, D.C.: U.S. Government Printing Office.

Westerman, Marty. March 1989. Death of the Frito bandito. *American Demographics*.

CHAPTER 8. MARKETING THROUGH SPORTS

Comte, Elizabeth. April 18, 1988. Coaches for sale. *Sports inc.*

Conklin, Michele. June 1986. Name your game. *Madison Avenue*.

Donaton, Scott. June 19, 1989. Senior Olympics offer marketers forceful finish. *Advertising Age*.

———. July 24, 1989. Infiniti serves first at U.S. Open: Nissan campaign starts early. *Advertising Age*.

Doyle, Thomas B. May 1988. Survival of the fittest. *American Demographics*.

Dunavant, Keith. June 12, 1989. Army-Navy game seeking corporate touch. *Sporting News*.

Durslag, Melvin. March 7, 1987. Watch the vaulter—and be sure to read the crossbar. *TV Guide*.

Fierman, Jaclyn. June 10, 1985. Companies pay for polo's cachet. *Fortune*.

Goulian, Lisa. April 18, 1988. Out of the gutter. *Sports inc.*

Johnson, William Oscar. July 1988. Sports and suds. *Sports Illustrated*.

Kellner, Jenny. May 8, 1989. Corporate sponsors find place in Derby field. *Sporting News*.

Konrad, Walecia. February 1, 1988. Will corporate sponsors get burned by the torch? *Business Week*.

Lichtenstein, Grace. April 1989. Days of glory. *Vogue*.

Macnow, Glen. June 5, 1989. Commercial plugs invade broadcasts. *Sporting News*.

————. June 26, 1989. Ueberroth's legacy: sponsorship bonanza. *Sporting News*.

Management Review. November 1988. Reebok's strategic alliances.

McGeehan, Patrick. February 1, 1988. Visa, Kodak big winners in Olympics. *Advertising Age*.

————. March 14, 1988. Sponsorships put icing on NHL's cake. *Advertising Age*.

McManus, John. July 31, 1989. The Goodwill Games: Ted Turner may get the last laugh. *Adweek*.

Meyers, Janet. July 10, 1989. Military maneuvering for sport sponsorships. *Advertising Age*.

Murphy, Brian. May 29, 1989. What makes those Indy cars go? Sponsors. *Sporting News*.

Oneal, Michael, et al. August 31, 1987. Nothing sells like sports. *Business Week*.

Seagren, Bob. September 15, 1989. Personal interview.

Sports inc. April 18, 1988. The $20-billion golf national product.

Stogel, Chuck. April 18, 1988. Running a tournament. *Sports inc*.

Time. December 7, 1987. The cost of being a sport.

Upton, Helen. August 29, 1989. Telephone interview.

Weinstein, Mindy. August 14, 1989. Dead stars are in. *Advertising Age*.

CHAPTER 9. CATCHING THE TIDE

American Demographics. June 1988. The gay market.

Arax, Mark. April 5, 1987. Asian influx alters life in suburbia. *Los Angeles Times*.

Bentley, Judith. 1981. *American immigration today—pressures, problems, policies*. New York: Julian Messner.

Carpenter, Larry. November 1987. How to market to regions. *American Demographics*.

Curtindale, Frieda. March 1989. A red-hot Mustang. *American Demographics*.

Daniel Yankelovich Group, Inc. Fall 1987. *The mature Americans—a study of today's men and women 50 years and over*.

EBONY. April 1989. The biggest secret of race relations: The new white minority.

Edmondson, Brad. January 1988. America's hot spots. *American Demographics*.

Erwin, Diana Griego. September 12, 1989. Gay festival reflects need for tolerance. *Orange County Register*.

Fortune. November 24, 1986. The super minority's poor cousins.

Hair, Jay. Spring 1989. Corporations and environmentalists synergy in action. *Windstar Journal*.

———. Spring 1989(B). Excerpts of remarks at Corporate Conservation Council Synergy Conference. *Windstar Journal*.

Harrell, James and Paul Armstrong. January 15, 1990. Going to Market in East Bloc. *Los Angeles Times/Orange County*.

Impact Resources, Inc. June 1989. *Asian consumers—special report*. Columbus, Ohio: Impact Resources.

Kern, Richard. May 1988. The Asian market: Too good to be true? *Sales & Marketing Management*.

Knight, Robin, and Eleni Dimmler. June 5, 1989. The greening of Europe's industries. *U.S. News & World Report*.

Kohut, Andrew, and James Shriver. May 17, 1989. Environment regaining a foothold on the national agenda. *Gallup Poll News Service*.

Lippert, Barbara. July 24, 1989. Levis recasts its rainbow coalition as the grand young party. *Adweek*.

Long, Kim. 1988. *The American forecaster 1989 almanac*. Philadelphia, Pa.: Running.

Maines, John. August 1988. Up where they belong. *American Demographics*.

Moore, Thomas. September 16, 1985. Different folks, different strokes. *Fortune*.

Naisbitt, John. 1984. *Megatrends*. New York: Warner.

Orange County Register. October 2, 1989.

Riche, Martha Farnsworth. March 1989. California here it comes. *American Demographics*.

Russell, Cheryl. February 1989. Guilty, as charged. *American Demographics*.

Schiffman, •Leon G., and Leslie Lazar Kanuk. May 17, 1987. A market's segments. *Marketing*.

Schwartz, Joe. May 1987. Military markets. *American Demographics*.

Shiver, Jube, Jr. January 15, 1990. At design lab, GM looks way down the road. *Los Angeles Times/Orange County*.

Silberner, Joanne. March 27, 1989. Protecting against one bad apple. *U.S. News & World Report*.

Takahashi, Dean. September 12, 1989. PX retailing does an about-face. *Orange County Register*.

Teinowitz, Ira. July 17, 1989. Jest plain offensive. *Advertising Age.*

Toffler, Alvin. 1980. *The third wave.* New York: William Morrow.

Tooley, Jo Ann, and Virginia Woltz. December 26, 1988. Leaving the office nest. *U.S. News & World Report.*

U.S. Bureau of the Census. October 1986. *1982 survey of minority-owned business enterprises—Asian Americans, American Indians, and other minorities.* Washington, D.C.: U.S. Government Printing Office.

————. 1988. Current population reports, series P-60, no. 161. *Money Income and Poverty Status in the United States: 1987.* (Advance data from the March 1988 current population survey.) Washington, D.C.: U.S. Government Printing Office.

U.S. Department of Defense. September/October 1988. *Defense 88 almanac.* Washington, D.C.: U.S. Government Printing Office.

Waldrop, Judith and Thomas Exter. January 1990. What the 1990 census will show. *American Demographics.*

Windstar Journal. Spring 1989.

Zelinsky, Wilbur. June 1989. Real regions. *American Demographics.*

GENERAL BIBLIOGRAPHY

Cruse, Harold. 1987. *Plural but equal*. New York: William Morrow.

Dychtwald, Ken. 1989. *Age wave*. Los Angeles: Jeremy P. Tarcher.

Naisbitt, John. 1984. *Megatrends*. New York: Warner.

Rapp, Stan, and Tom Collins. 1988. *MaxiMarketing*. New York: New American Library.

Riding, Alan. 1985. *Distant neighbors—portrait of the Mexicans*. New York: Random House.

Weinstein, Art. 1987. *Market segmentation*. Chicago: Probus.

INDEX

About the Author

CHESTER A. SWENSON is Founder and President of Marketing & Financial Management Enterprises, a well-know segmented marketing firm with offices in California, Michigan, and Texas. His numerous articles on market segmentation and life-style marketing have appeared in such publications as *Journal of Business Strategy*, *American Demographics*, *Management Review*, and the *Los Angeles Business Journal*.

TITLES OF INTEREST IN MARKETING, DIRECT MARKETING, AND SALES PROMOTION

For further information or a current catalog, write:
NTC Business Books
a division of *NTC Publishing Group*
4255 West Touhy Avenue
Lincolnwood, Illinois 60646-1975 U.S.A.